Cambridge

Elements in Ancient Egypt in Context
edited by
Gianluca Miniaci
University of Pisa
Juan Carlos Moreno García
CNRS, Paris
Anna Stevens
University of Cambridge and Monash University

MMXXI

EGYPT AND THE DESERT

John Coleman Darnell
Yale University

CAMBRIDGE
UNIVERSITY PRESS

CAMBRIDGE
UNIVERSITY PRESS

University Printing House, Cambridge CB2 8BS, United Kingdom

One Liberty Plaza, 20th Floor, New York, NY 10006, USA

477 Williamstown Road, Port Melbourne, VIC 3207, Australia

314–321, 3rd Floor, Plot 3, Splendor Forum, Jasola District Centre,
New Delhi – 110025, India

79 Anson Road, #06–04/06, Singapore 079906

Cambridge University Press is part of the University of Cambridge.

It furthers the University's mission by disseminating knowledge in the pursuit of education, learning, and research at the highest international levels of excellence.

www.cambridge.org
Information on this title: www.cambridge.org/9781108820530
DOI: 10.1017/9781108900683

First published 2021

A catalogue record for this publication is available from the British Library.

ISBN 978-1-108-82053-0 Paperback
ISSN 2516-4813 (online)
ISSN 2516-4805 (print)

Egypt and the Desert

Elements in Ancient Egypt in Context

DOI: 10.1017/9781108900683
First published online: May 2021

John Coleman Darnell
Yale University

Author for correspondence: John Coleman Darnell, john.darnell@yale.edu

Abstract: Deserts, the Red Land, bracket the narrow strip of alluvial Black Land that borders the Nile. Networks of desert roads ascended to the high desert from the Nile Valley, providing access to the mineral wealth and Red Sea ports of the Eastern Desert, as well as the oasis depressions and trade networks of the Western Desert. A historical perspective from the Predynastic through the Roman Periods highlights how developments in the Nile Valley altered the Egyptian administration and exploitation of the deserts. For the ancient Egyptians, the deserts were a living landscape, and at numerous points along the desert roads, they employed rock art and rock inscriptions to create and mark places. Such sites provide considerable evidence for the origin of writing in northeast Africa, the religious significance of the desert and expressions of personal piety, and the development of the early alphabet.

Keywords: Egypt, deserts, writing, administration, roads

ISBNs: 9781108820530 (PB), 9781108900683 (OC)
ISSNs: 2516-4813 (online), 2516-4805 (print)

Contents

1 The Red Land

The ancient Egyptians conceptualized their world as a series of balanced pairs, even opposites, held in equilibrium by the force of *maat*, cosmic order and rectitude. The duality of the diurnal and nocturnal solar cycle corresponded to the annual opposites of the north to south and south to north journey of the sun, and the yearly round of the high and low Niles. Geographically, the major divisions of the ordered world could appear as Upper Egypt and Lower Egypt, the southern and northern realms over which the king ruled as "Lord of the Two Lands"; the Nilotic world could also take the form of eastern and western divisions as the Two Banks. An equally significant pairing was *Kemet,* the Black Land, the extent of the rich alluvial soil, and *Deshret,* the Red Land, the vast deserts that stretched east and west of the Nile Valley. One could be a short distance out in the desert, with a clear view of the green ribbons of cultivation flanking the shimmering blue band of the Nile (Figure 1), and still describe a walk to that cultivation as "going down to the Black Land" – as "hill country" was synonymous with "desert" and "foreign land," an immense and conceptually outer realm was but a stone's throw from the waters of the Nile flood.

In the fifth century BCE, the Greek historian Herodotus applied to Egypt the now hoary designation "the gift of the Nile." Indeed, ancient Egyptian civilization would never have attained attained the heights of achievement to which it rose without the reliable water source and relatively predictable flooding of the river. Herodotus was correct that the black alluvial soil – the substance of which the Black Land is composed – was a literal gift of the Nile inundation. Modern historians and Egyptologists alike sometimes take Herodotus's characterization too far, however, assuming that ancient Egypt was all but exclusively the narrow strip of alluvium bordering the Nile. Some have suggested that the ancient Egyptians avoided the deserts except when mining or military expeditions forced them reluctantly into the rocky and sandy barrenness. In the minds of some recent authors, the deserts bordering the Nile Valley were realms of terror and chaos for the ancient Egyptians.[1] As archaeology and epigraphy have revealed, with increasing clarity over the past several decades, the truth of ancient Egypt's relationship with the Eastern and Western Deserts was far from random, insignificant, or fearful.

Marching along the outer edges of Middle Kingdom hunting scenes at Beni Hasan, griffins and other imaginary creatures mark the outer edges of the already outer desert regions (Gerke, 2014). At the rim of the world that the far corner of the tomb wall mirrors, the desert beasts that are the hunter's quarry eventually become the mythical creatures that might populate the twilight lands

---

[1] Keimer, 1944; Aufrère, 2007: 139; Quack, 2010: 349; Lazaridis, 2019: 129.

Figure 1 At the site of Moalla, looking across the Nile and its narrow bands of
cultivation to the western escarpment

at the rims of the horizons. Yet fantastic fauna are relatively rare at desert rock
inscription sites (Darnell, 2013a: 68–69) – even at a remote desert pass the
Egyptians apparently did not feel themselves to be approaching a dangerous
liminal region, nor do they seem to have feared such creatures as aspects of real
desert travel. Even in those Beni Hasan scenes in which the hunter – through the
presence of desert monsters – might appear to brag about hunting at the ends of
the earth, the monstrous beings wear collars. The desert might eventually
become truly uncanny if one journeyed far enough, but the desert prowess of
the ancient Egyptians seems to have led them to believe that any such monsters
could be incorporated into a rational and practical, inhabited desert environment. Desert monsters, like the deserts themselves, could be domesticated.

Most of the mobile hunter-gatherer groups who roamed the seasonally moist
eastern Sahara, accompanied by expanding herds of cattle and caprids by ca.
6000 BCE, began to settle down to lives of farming and herding under the
influence of a drying climate around 5000 BCE (Riemer, 2007). Although the
deserts went from center to periphery, the Nile Valley dwellers never entirely
left the drying hinterlands of the river and oases. Ancient Egyptians exploited
the vast geological and mineralogical wealth of the Eastern Desert, and utilized
the oases of the Western Desert of Egypt and Nubia as hubs for far-flung caravan

travel. Far from being empty terra incognita, the ancient Egyptian deserts were highly interconnected regions crisscrossed by well-marked and intensively traveled tracks, with numerous oasis settlements and high desert campsites revealing evidence of the products of Mediterranean and North African commerce. During the three millennia of pharaonic history, the Egyptians maintained a desert infrastructure of varying complexity, with bureaucratic offices to oversee the smooth functioning of inhabited desert areas and the caravans passing through them. A history of Egypt or Nubia that excludes the Red Land is but a fragment of the entire story of Egyptian and Nubian cultures.

The formal self-presentation of a late Old Kingdom administrator illustrates some of the derring-do and remarkable achievements of ancient Egyptians in the Western Desert, and demonstrates how the results of recent archaeological and epigraphic work have improved our understanding of Egyptian desert activity. The Sixth Dynasty governor of the First Nome (district) of Upper Egypt, Harkhuf, commissioned an "autobiography" for the façade of his tomb on the west bank of modern Aswan, site of his capital city and the traditional border between pharaonic Egypt and Nubia. Harkhuf served under kings Merenre (ca. 2287–2278 BCE) and during the boyhood of his successor, Pepi II (who would reign an unprecedented 94 years, ca. 2278–2184 BCE). In his text, Harkhuf relates his journeys south into Nubia; in two of his exploratory and trading expeditions, Harkhuf's goal was a now-obscure southern territory called Yam, ultimately linked to Egypt by two routes: the Elephantine Road, departing from Gebel Tingar on the west bank of Aswan, just south of Harkhuf's tomb, and the Oasis Road, whose Nile terminus was in the Thinite Nome (the district of Abydos, the terminus to the road being close to modern Girga).

The length of his itinerary, and the Lower Nubian toponyms that Harkhuf lists for his return journey, have led to an Egyptological equation of Yam with the region of the Third Cataract of the Nile or further south, near the Fifth Cataract (O'Connor, 1986). For over two decades, the Theban Desert Road Survey (Yale University) has mapped and studied much of the Oasis Road, called the Girga Road after its major Nilotic terminus, and the ACACIA Project (University of Cologne) has traced Old Kingdom activity along the Abu Ballas Trail, connecting Dakhla Oasis with Gebel Uweinat to the southwest, near the juncture of the modern states of Egypt, Sudan, and Libya, roughly 580 kilometers southwest of Balat in Dakhla Oasis and 650 kilometers due west of the Nile. Combining archaeological work and epigraphic recording, these surveys have revealed physical evidence for Old Kingdom expeditions utilizing the Oasis Road and branches thereof leading to the far southwest, offering clues to Harkhuf's ultimate destination in Yam. Harkhuf departed the region of Abydos via the Girga Road, on a Theban branch of which is a rock inscription of the cartouche of a Sixth Dynasty king Pepi. He then traveled on to Kharga Oasis, past campsites now known to have functioned during the Fifth Dynasty; Harkhuf may have continued westward in his journey, arriving at the Old Kingdom outpost of Balat in Dakhla Oasis, ultimately traveling to the southwest along the Abu Ballas Trail toward Gebel Uweinat.

An inscription from the reign of Montuhotep II (ca. 2055–2004 BCE) at Gebel Uweinat, discovered in 2008, depicts the enthroned Eleventh Dynasty ruler receiving tribute from the lands of Yam and Tekhebet. While not necessarily in the territory of Yam itself, the inscription suggests that Yam was not exclusively a Nilotic location, but rather at least to some extent a region of the Western Desert, perhaps beyond Kharga and Dakhla Oases (Cooper, 2012). The inscription of Montuhotep II indicates that Egyptian missions to Uweinat received *sntr* – incense – from Yam. Increasing aridity in the Sahara ultimately restricted the movements of pastoral groups, perhaps contributing to the ultimate obsolescence of the toponym. Ongoing archaeological surveys, new epigraphic discoveries, and a resulting reappraisal of long-known hieroglyphic texts offer exciting insights into Egypt in the Eastern Sahara.

1.1 Desert Roads

The common Egyptian term for the desert, *ḫꜣs.t*, was written with the hieroglyphic sign of three desert hills, with valleys in between. Most of Egypt is in fact a desert, cut through by dry water courses, wadis in Arabic. Wherever water was plentiful, in the Nile Valley or a desert oasis, that water source was for the most part in a valley or depression, since the vast region of northeast Africa is otherwise a high desert. The ancient Egyptians could therefore encapsulate the essence of a desert journey in the phrase "going up and going down" (Darnell, 2003: 82–84). The desert terrain frequently necessitates steep ascents, suitable for human travelers and the donkeys that served as the main pack animals of the pharaonic era (Förster, 2015: 385–406) (Figure 2). Donkeys carry the greatest load per pound of any beast of burden available to the ancient Egyptians, and are particularly well adapted for desert travel, able to tolerate both moderate dehydration and poor quality forage (Förster, 2015: 428–434). The introduction of the camel as a major means of transport around the middle of the first millennium BCE required roads with more gradual ascents, but the camel's ability to go without water for extended periods allowed for more widely spaced water sources. Desert roads of pharaonic date presupposed the existence of frequent food and water depots, even cisterns or wells, with the associated administrative oversight of traffic, systems of fortifications (Vogel, 2004; Vogel, 2013), and the patrolling of roads.

Figure 2 Ancient track from Aswan descending into Kurkur Oasis; inset: rock inscription of a donkey carrying a pack, from the Wadi Hilal (east of Elkab)

The Nile was not an ideal route of travel and transport year round. During the low Nile, sandbanks would have barred all but those vessels with the shallowest of drafts, while the season of the inundation would have seen the channel of the river lost beneath the muddy waters that stretched out like an inland sea from desert edge to desert edge (Bonneau, 1964). A series of rocky cataracts beginning at Aswan and continuing at intervals to just south of Meroe, and bends of the river in which both current and wind might oppose a voyage, could also discourage a total reliance on the river as a corridor for trade (Darnell, 2013a: 40–42). Although a vessel could be dragged around a cataract – and indeed an ancient slipway for hauling boats through the desert bordering the Second Cataract is known from Mirgissa[2] – a donkey caravan could more easily transport cargo past a cataract or other obstruction. Any north-south track in the cultivated land would have encountered a bewildering array of larger and smaller irrigation canals, making travel difficult. A caravan on a desert road, paralleling the Nile in the near desert, might be preferable to a trip on or near the Nile. For journeys to the east or the west, desert roads alone provide access.

---

[2] Vercoutter, 1970: 13–15, 173–180, 204–214. The tomb of Amunhotep, called Huy (Theban Tomb 40), depicts boats being hauled over a muddy surface, perhaps a similar use of a slipway (Davies, 1926).

An ancient Egyptian road is most often a set of slightly meandering, parallel tracks, where the traffic of human feet and donkey hooves has pushed aside the rocks and pebbles of the desert surface (Bubenzer & Bolten, 2013: 69–71). Those grooves remain visible for millennia, and are further marked by pot sherds, the remains of broken ceramic storage containers and cooking vessels (Figure 3).[3] The desert surface normally required no further human augmentation, with some exceptional cases. The ancient Egyptians could engineer impressive built roads to access quarries, providing an even surface for the transportation of large stones (Shaw, 2006; 2010: 109–124). A twelve kilometer long paved road, consistently two meters wide, connects the basalt quarry at Widan el-Faras (at the northern edge of the Fayum depression) with a now vanished lake (Harrell, 2002: 235–336). A built roadway accessing the Hatnub quarry also employed dry-stone causeways to maintain an even grade when crossing wadis (Shaw, 2013). Cleared tracks could connect desert locales: a route between Dashur and the Fayum may have served as both a quarry road and military highway (Shaw, 2010: 118–19); an eighty kilometer cleared road connected the Gebel el-Asr quarries with the Nile at Toshka (Murray, 1939); paved and cleared tracks are also associated with quarries in the First Cataract region (Storemyr, et al., 2013).

Travelers, from kings and their retinues to police patrols to priests and scribes, recorded their names, and often much else, when roads passed an area of stone suitable for carving. Rock art and rock inscriptions complement

Figure 3 Ancient caravan tracks west of the Wadi Abu Medawi ascent; inset: "broken ceramics on the road," two views of the dense ceramics on the Wadi Alamat Road

---

[3] The ancient Egyptians recognized the dichotomy between desert surface and the broken ceramics on the roads as "gravel of the desert and broken pots in the road" (D. Darnell, 2002: 156).

ceramic evidence from the roads, allowing a combination of archaeology and epigraphy to plot changes in desert administration. Desert rock inscriptions also reveal historical episodes otherwise unattested in Nile Valley sources, from an early Dynasty 0 ruler's defeat of an enemy, to the interactions between Middle Kingdom Dakhla and desert tribes, to Montuhotep II's far-flung expedition to Gebel Uweinat. The deserts preserve considerable evidence for religious practices, from the transformation of natural features into sacred spaces to some of the earliest attested expressions of personal piety. The uninhabited desert allowed individuals to transcend standards of decorum expected in monuments along the banks of the Nile.

1.2 Geographic Overview of the Egyptian Deserts and Road Networks

No matter how level the plateau across which an ancient Egyptian desert road traveled, inevitably almost all desert arteries would focus on a narrow pass at the escarpment leading to or from one of the water-rich depressions in which most major settlements would be situated. These passes connected the high desert plateau with the low desert border of the Nile Valley, the floor of the oasis depressions of the Western Desert, a mining or quarrying site within a valley of the Eastern Desert, or the shore of the Red Sea far to the east. Such points for ascending and descending the plateau were more easily controlled than the broad expanses of high desert, across which the parallel paths of a desert track might spread for a width of a kilometer or more. Termed a "narrow door" by the ancient Egyptians (Darnell, et al., 2002: 35–36), the desert choke point of a road pass could be open, or it might be blocked by human agency[4] as well as a lack of water.[5] Although the Satire of the Trades (Jäger, 2004: 144–145) suggests that the state of a pass or the security of a longer stretch of road could be one of the concerns that troubled the traveling courier (*sḫȝḫ.ty*), a properly administered road could be safe (Brunner, 1937: 43–44).

Mapping the desert roads of ancient Egypt is a process still in its initial phases. The ancient Egyptians themselves mounted exploratory missions to seek out new routes, yet only one significant desert map survives. Not all tracks on which ancient remains are present were in use at all periods of Egyptian history, and several texts reference the ancient Egyptians' own exploration of routes, blazing new trails for trade, with officials securing oasis territory and searching out its populations (Darnell, et al., 2002: 73; Förster, 2015: 269–276). A unique Twentieth Dynasty

---

[4] *Cf.* Wadi Hammamat inscription no. 17, ll. 11–13 (Couyat & Montet, 1912: pl. 5 and p. 40); Darnell, 2008: 89–90.

[5] An inscription of Seti I at Kanais (in the Wadi Mia) states that prior to the well dug under Seti's orders, the route was blocked (Schott, 1961: text A, ll. 2–3).

papyrus (reign of Ramesses IV, ca. 1153–1147 BCE) with a map of a portion of the Wadi Hammamat shows how the ancient Egyptians recorded tracks, water sources, and their own monuments (e.g., a stela of Seti I, ca. 1294–1279 BCE) in the landscape (Harrell & Brown, 1992).[6]

Maps of principally the nineteenth and twentieth centuries CE show a number of routes then in use in the Egyptian and Nubian deserts, and some more detailed descriptions of itineraries were published before all of those routes passed out of use (an excellent example is Gleichen, 1905). More recent travelers and researchers have mapped and described desert roads (Riemer & Förster, 2013), and remote sensing techniques are being developed to combine historical map data with satellite imagery to identify the most promising areas for desert road surveys (Bubenzer & Bolton, 2013; Gasperini & Pethen, 2018). Ultimately, however, ancient tracks can be securely identified only through the physical collection of artifacts, and the recording of rock art and inscriptions requires intensive survey followed by photography and epigraphic drawings. Digital techniques have streamlined the epigraphic process, enabling entire sites and their hinterlands to be recorded in a season of work (Darnell, Darnell, & Urcia, 2018); in combination with three-dimensional modeling, such recording techniques provide a better understanding of inscription sites within the broader context of desert road archaeology.

Although a definitive description of ancient roads in Egypt is not possible, several important networks of routes and associated sites are known. The maps accompanying this Element (Maps 1–5) focus on major road networks, and include all of the major routes and toponyms mentioned herein. Many other tracks and important passes – such as those at the eastern escarpment of Kharga Oasis (Giddy, 1987: map 2) – have been omitted altogether. The following sketches of roads, and the maps that illustrate them, should provide a broad overview, and a background for more detailed study.

The Western Desert of Egypt – the Eastern Sahara from an African perspective – is bounded on the north by the Mediterranean Sea. By the reign of Ramesses II (ca. 1279–1213 BCE), fortresses guarded the desert roads that paralleled the coast (see Section 2.5). The waterless expanses of the Qattara Depression were a barrier to desert travel, so that the next viable route to the south that leads into the Nile Valley began in Siwa Oasis. During the second half of the first millennium BCE, Siwa became the latest of the Western Desert oases to be incorporated into the pharaonic state. Although Siwa may be mentioned as part of the trajectory of a combined Libyan and Sea Peoples invasion during the reign of Merneptah (ca. 1208 BCE), it was at the very edge of the "oasis ring,"

---

[6] https://collezionepapiri.museoegizio.it/en-GB/document/9/ (accessed 10/1/2020).

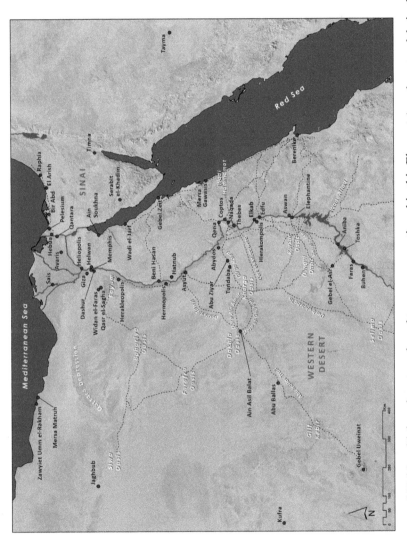

Map 1 Map of Egypt and Nubia with key desert roads and toponyms mentioned in this Element (map layout and design by Alberto Urcia)

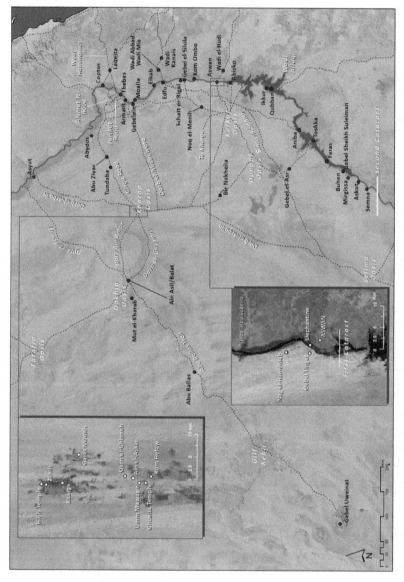

Map 2 Map of Upper Egypt, Lower Nubia, and the Western Desert oases, with key desert roads and toponyms mentioned in this Element (map layout and design by Alberto Urcia)

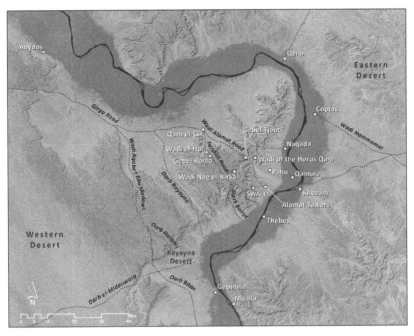

Map 3 Major roads, military installations, caravansaries, inscription sites, and Nilotic settlements in the Qena Bend of the Nile (map layout and design by Alberto Urcia)

interconnected caravan routes that traveled through well-watered depressions (Willeitner, 2003). From Siwa, a long route to the south passes through Kufra Oasis to Gebel Uweinat, and thence past a string of wells to el-Fasher, and on to the White Nile south of Khartoum (compare the route of Hassanein Bey, 1925: map opposite p. 8; for the trans-Saharan routes, see Thiry, 1995).

The "oasis ring" links the Fayum, Bahariya, Farafra, Dakhla, and Kharga Oases with points in the Nile Valley. From the Delta or northern Middle Egypt, a traveler beginning in the Fayum could use a desert road that led southwest to Bahariya Oasis; from Bahariya, routes continued on to Farafra Oasis, the major oasis farthest from the Nile; from Farafra, travelers could make a southerly arc through Dakhla and Kharga Oases. From Dakhla, the Abu Ballas Trail accessed points to the far southwest; alternatively, passing through Kharga, a traveler could return to the Upper Egyptian Nile Valley along the Girga Road or head south, along a network of desert roads that connected small oases and accessed the Nubian Nile Valley.

Routes in Middle Egypt linked that region of the Nile Valley with both the Western and Eastern Deserts, although the periods during which certain tracks functioned await further archaeological confirmation. The famous Darb el-

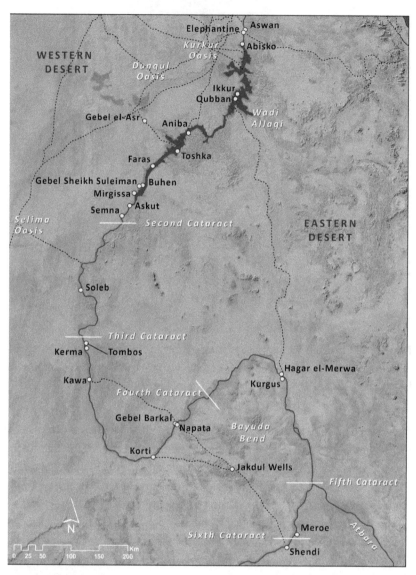

Map 4 Map of Nubia, including Nilotic sites and important desert roads, along with oases and smaller areas of wells (map layout and design by Alberto Urcia)

Arba'in, the "Forty (Days) Road," connected Asyut, via Kharga and smaller wells and oases, with el-Fasher in Darfur. By the Middle Ages, this road was essential to trade in northeastern Africa, the route for caravans transporting salt, luxury goods, and slaves (Riemer & Förster, 2013: 52–53). The entire route of a pharaonic Darb el-Arba'in remains uncertain, although a north-south track through Kharga, active from ca. 1700 to 1100 BCE, reveals that at least

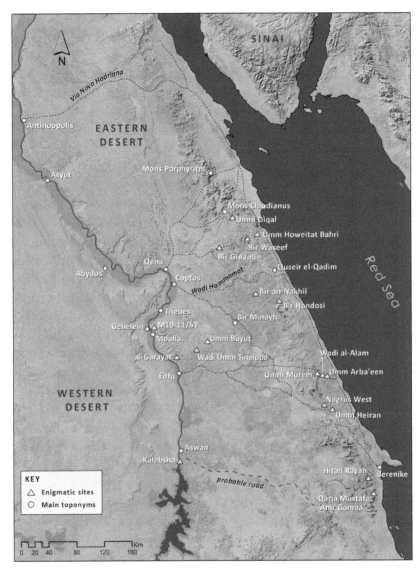

Map 5 Map of the Eastern Desert of Egypt, with key sites and roads in use during the Roman Period (map layout and design by Alberto Urcia)

a portion of the Darb el-Arba'in functioned by the time of the Second Intermediate Period (Darnell & Darnell, 2016: 63–64). Provincial leaders in Middle Egypt, particularly in the region of Beni Hasan and Deir el-Bersha, exploited routes into the Eastern Desert that provided further connections north to the Levant and south to Nubia (Moreno Garcia, 2017). Even without identifying specific routes into Middle Egypt, textual and pictorial records in Middle

Kingdom tombs highlight how trade with pastoral populations in the Western Desert enhanced the wealth of those provinces (Moreno Garcia, 2017: 116–117).

The region known as the Qena Bend, roughly stretching from Nag Hammadi to Armant, is the cynosure of desert roads in southern Egypt. The shortest route linking the oases of the Western Desert with the Nile Valley is the Girga Road – Harkhuf's Oasis Road – that ascends the northern escarpment of Kharga Oasis and descends into the Nile Valley north of the Qena Bend, with branches cutting across that bend and continuing on to Naqada and Thebes (Darnell, with D. Darnell, 2013). The shortest road between the Red Sea and the Nile Valley enters the latter in the vicinity of Coptos, passing through the Wadi Hammamat, from which the track derives its most common name (Gasse, 2016). As with the Girga Road, the Wadi Hammamat Road has a Theban terminus, with a branch of the Wadi Hammamat Road – via the well of Laqeita – leading further south to Khozam, on the northern border of Thebes. During the First Intermediate Period, Upper Egyptian nomarchs attempted to exploit numerous local routes, whereas the later, central administration would prioritize a development of fewer routes with higher traffic and more intensive economic functions.

In the southwestern desert of Egypt, the small oasis of Kurkur was the hub of roads that connected the region of Aswan with southern Kharga Oasis as well as points to the south (D. Darnell & Darnell, 2013). Two major north-south routes passing Kurkur Oasis, the Darb Gallaba and Darb Bitan, accessed the Qena Bend directly, paralleling the Nile and potentially bypassing any Nilotic control between Aswan and Thebes. The Darb Bitan, ascending the plateau to the west of Armant and passing through the long Wadi Abu Madawi, could bypass major Nilotic settlements altogether, and access the Girga Road in the vicinity of Farshut. Tracks leading from Kurkur and passing through Dunqul Oasis run just to the west of one of the few major quarries in the Western Desert at Gebel el-Asr (also known as the "Chephren Diorite Quarries"), where the Egyptians extracted anorthosite gneiss, carnelian, and jasper (Shaw, et al., 2010).

The desert of the Sinai Peninsula and the Negev was an important source for copper, malachite, and turquoise. In addition to the land route across the Sinai – the "Ways of Horus" (see Section 2.5) – harbors on the western shore of the Gulf of Suez supported sea-borne traffic.[7] Quarry roads in the Eastern Desert accessed the wealth of stones from the Precambrian Basement exposed in the Red Sea mountains, some quarries in use from Early Dynastic times, others exploited predominantly in the Roman Period (e.g.,

---

[7] Archaeological work at Ayn Soukhna and Wadi el-Jarf, and Mersa/Wadi Gawasis has revealed further information about the Red Sea in the pharaonic period; summaries of the results of those missions are Tallet, 2016; Tallet and Mahfouz, 2012; Bard and Fattovich, 2018.

Mons Porphyrites and Mons Claudianus) (Klemm & Klemm, 2008: 269–314). The Wadi Hammamat road accessed the mineral resources of that wadi system and provided a route for the transportation of ship parts for Red Sea trade.

The great valley network of the Wadi Abbad/Wadi Mia, which leads from the Eastern Desert highlands into the region of Edfu, was the avenue for accessing the gold mines of the southeastern Egyptian desert, and provided another route to the Red Sea. In the Eastern Desert of Nubia some of the most important road networks were those that accessed the gold mining region of the Wadi Allaqi. During the Napatan and Meroitic period, the "King's Road" cut across the Bayuda Bend of the Nile, connecting the capitals of Napata and Meroe (Lohwasser, 2013). By the Roman Period, a dense network of roads in the Eastern Desert connected the Nile Valley with mines, quarries, and the Red Sea coast, with an infrastructure of watch-towers, wells, and fortresses (Sidebotham, 2011: 125–174).

1.3 Water Resources

In any desert travel, water was of perennial concern. Old and Middle Kingdom water depots along desert roads (Figure 4) consisted of large, ceramic storage jars that could be regularly replenished with donkey-borne leather water skins (Förster, 2015: 435–447; Köpp-Junk, Riemer, & Förster, 2017). In the Eastern Desert, Middle Kingdom rulers ordered the excavation of wells along the Wadi Hammamat road (Couyat & Montet, 1912: 83 and pl. 31, ll. 13–14), while New Kingdom pharaohs opened wells in wadis accessing the southeastern gold mines (Franzmeier, 2010). In the Western Desert, a large cistern occupied the midpoint of the Girga Road between the Nile Valley and Kharga Oasis, during the Seventeenth Dynasty, a hydraulic installation that continued in use through the New Kingdom (Darnell, with D. Darnell, 2013: 247–251). The innovative underground *qanat* irrigation system, introduced by the time of the Persian Period (Twenty Seventh Dynasty, 525–404 BCE), revolutionized cultivation in the oases (see Section 2.6).

Around the cusp of the Third and Fourth Dynasties, the ancient Egyptians began construction of a massive reservoir dam (the Sadd el-Kafara) in the Wadi Garawi, east of modern Helwan (Garbrecht & Bertram, 1983). This structure, one of the earliest known monumental dam constructions in the world, appears, in spite of its over-engineering, to have been abandoned before completion. No other remains of similar dams are known from the Eastern or Western Desert, and the combination of water depots, wells, and cisterns fulfilled the needs of desert travelers, caravans, and military expeditions.

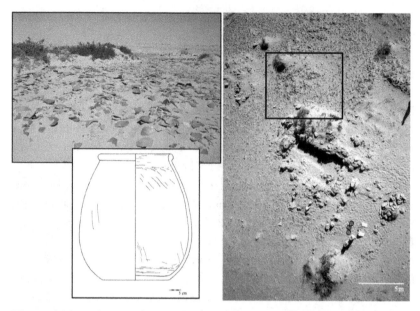

Figure 4 View (from aerial photography kite) of the Middle Kingdom desert outpost, Abu Ziyar, along the Girga Road; insets: dense concentration of sherds from water storage jars, as in the reconstructed vessel (ca. 1950 BCE)

1.4 About This Element

Egypt and the desert – each is a topic of supreme interest and immense scope. The desert was not a blank space, bounded by inhabited areas. The study of Egypt stretches over a vast expanse of time from its cultural origins in the North African Neolithic through its rise, floruit, and entry into the realm of legend. An investigation of the Eastern and Western Deserts encompasses an immense space bordering the Mediterranean, the Red Sea and Indian Oceans, and a desert stretching west toward the Atlantic, a great inland sea of sand and rock linking cultures on a global scale. In order to approach such a grand subject, one that defies easy simplification, this Element will emphasize the Predynastic and Pharaonic Periods of Egypt, stressing the intersection of epigraphic and archaeological evidence. An in-depth analysis of all the cultures, ethnicities, and interconnections across the Egyptian and Saharan realms is impossible in such a concise format; this Element focuses on how the Egyptian state integrated desert territories into its political and economic spheres of influence, and examines how the ancient Egyptians viewed the desert as a living entity in their cosmology, and a participant in rituals. Much work remains to be done regarding the interconnections between the farther, "Libyan" Western Desert and Nubia (Moreno Garcia, 2018), a topic but briefly addressed here. In order to limit references, the current work cites many of the author's own works, for the most part as sources for additional bibliography. Dates given in the current work are based, for consistency, on Shaw, 2000.

Section 2 provides a chronological overview of Egyptian interactions with the desert frontiers, from the Predynastic through the late Roman Period, emphasizing administrative developments, especially the repeated appearance of dual systems of oversight, and the incorporation of outer regions into the Egyptian state. Four millennia of ancient Egyptian desert policy provide fruitful avenues of comparison for scholars of other ancient civilizations and associated frontier regions. Section 3 turns to the ontological status of the desert, its identity as a numinous landscape, and its liminal state as a conduit for communion with the divine. In Section 4 the extensive corpora of Predynastic rock art in the Eastern and Western Deserts reveal an evolution of iconographic syntax that culminates in the nascent hieroglyphic script. Section 5 examines the self-presentation of foreigners in the deserts of Egypt, including the expression of a persistent Nubian identity, and the development of the Early Alphabetic script through interactions of Egyptians and their neighbors to the northeast.

2 The Deserts and Their Administration

Rather than providing merely an ever expanding and changing gazetteer of sites and toponyms, the history of ancient Egyptian activities in the Eastern and Western Deserts reveals the development of a bureaucratic approach to administering and integrating areas beyond the Egyptian Nile Valley. Following the earliest expressions of royal authority in the deserts during Dynasty 0, the Early Dynastic Period sees the application of sigillographic imagery to official control of the desert economy. By the late Old Kingdom, apparently highly centralized authority over desert activities developed into a bipartite system of administration, in which royal representatives oversaw expeditions in cooperation with officials of a relevant bureaucratic office. As the early Middle Kingdom began to incorporate formerly outer regions into the central state, inhabitants of the oasis regions of the Western Desert and Lower Nubia became increasingly important agents of control.

The Egyptian approach to desert regions never relied on defined border fortifications, although forts and fortified towns guarded entry points into the Nile Valley (Morris, 2005). The expression of royal authority and state control traveled along the linear structures of roads, and the administration of nodes along itineraries was dominant in the expression of Egyptian hegemony outside of the Nile Valley. The "Wall of the Ruler" in the northeastern Delta (Vögel, 2004: 19, 39, 161ff., 167ff.) designated a constellation of outposts, and a reference on a stela of Tutankhamun to a "Western Wall" in the region of the Sinn el-Kiddab appears to allude to a system of patrols rather than any major structure (see Section 2.5).

Through the first millennium BCE, the several – often non-Egyptian – dynasties that controlled the Nile Valley maintained and even expanded on earlier desert road networks. Following an apparent diminution of official activity during the late Ramesside Period, the Twenty-First Dynasty sees an increased emphasis on the oases of the Western Desert; the oases will remain important foci of official attention, especially following innovations in irrigation during the Persian Period. The Eastern Desert quarries are intensively exploited during the Ptolemaic and Roman Periods, with Red Sea ports linking Egypt with the increasing trade of the Red Sea and Indian Ocean. During the Late Roman Period, innovation continues, with the appearance of a new sort of desert settlement in the central Eastern Desert, apparently an economic and administrative counterpart to the monastic communities of the Western Desert, both systems of desert control replacing earlier oversight based at the once powerful temple establishments. In the Eastern Desert the Blemmyes (an important desert-dwelling group that controlled much of Upper Egypt and Lower Nubia during the Late Roman Period) created a built environment far greater than any previous groups indigenous to the Egyptian deserts.

2.1 Protodynastic and Early Dynastic Organization of the Desert (ca. 3250–2686 BCE): The Deserts Become Outer Regions

From the fifth millennium BCE, Badarian and Tasian cultural material is known from desert sites in the Western Desert in the environs of Dakhla, at Kurkur Oasis, in the Qena Bend, in the central Eastern Desert, and at Bir Umm Tineidba east of Elkab.[8] The Badarian-Tasian culture, with its own desert connections, finds a more distant counterpart in the Bashendi Culture in Dakhla Oasis. As the Nile Valley of Egypt and Nubia became an increasing focus of social, economic, and political developments during the late fifth millennium BCE, the rise of the Naqada cultures in Upper Egypt and the A-Group in Lower Nubia saw the beginning of cultural and iconographic features that ultimately lead in a direct line of development into what we recognize as pharaonic Egypt. The Sheikh Muftah culture, also focused on Dakhla Oasis and apparently associated with a nomadic lifestyle, persisted through the time of the Predynastic Period and

---

[8] For the Badarian-Tasian culture and the late Neolithic in the Egyptian deserts, see the discussions and references in D. Darnell, 2002, 156–169; D. Darnell and Darnell, 2013; Wuttmann, et al., 2012; Gatto, 2013; Horn, 2017; Dachy, et al., 2018.

through the Old Kingdom, finally becoming fully subsumed in an Egyptian oasis culture by the beginning of the Middle Kingdom (Riemer, 2011; Warfe & Ricketts, 2019).

As cultures based in the Nile Valley came to dominate northeast Africa during the fourth millennium BCE, official interest in the desert hinterland of the Nile Valley and its routes is in evidence from the time of the creation of an Upper Egyptian state. While regional power centers are in evidence from the Naqada II Period (ca. 3500–3250 BCE), a line of rulers, commonly called "Dynasty 0," appears to have overseen a unified Upper Egypt from ca. 3250 BCE until ca. 3100 BCE. One of these Dynasty 0 rulers inscribed a monumental hieroglyphic inscription on a desert cliff at el-Khawy, near Elkab (see Section 4.3). The rising dominance of tableaux of royal ritual power in the rock art of Upper Egypt already during the late Predynastic Period (see Section 4) may be evidence of an attempt to bring desert activities increasingly under the control of local rulers, and later, a nascent kingship.

The nature of Early Dynastic expeditions in the deserts remains uncertain (Wilkinson, 1999: 162–176; Hamilton, 2016; 2019). Rock inscriptions from the First and Second Dynasties at Wadi Ameyra in south Sinai reveal that officials administering foreign territories and those representing the palace were both directly involved in exploiting the resources of Sinai (Tallet, 2015a: 38–42; Tallet, 2015b). On Upper Egyptian desert roads the abundance of Early Dynastic *serekhs* – each the hieroglyphic representation of a quadrangular enclosure in which the Horus name of a ruler was written – suggests royal economic oversight of the deserts, their products and trade (see Section 4.4).

2.2 The Old Kingdom in the Egyptian Deserts (ca. 2686–2160 BCE): Expressions of Egyptian Domination in the Outer Regions

A number of rock inscriptions and archaeological sites attest to mining and military expeditions moving through the deserts during the Old Kingdom, with more general trade and travel also occurring along several defined routes.[9] Some early officials bore naval titles, revealing a connection between nautical navigation and traveling the seas of rock and sand bordering the Nile Valley (Tallet & Sauzeau, 2018). A number of Old Kingdom titles describe control of roads and desert outposts, indicating the construction of a physical infrastructure in the deserts (Eichler, 1993: 202–203; Moreno Garcia, 2013: 101). On the Red Sea littoral, the Old Kingdom constructed a harbor at Wadi el-Jarf, with a corresponding circular fortification on the coast of Sinai (Tallet & Marouard,

---

[9] For overviews of Old Kingdom activity in the Eastern and Western Deserts, see Tallet, 2018: 85–138; Sweeney, 2014; Förster, 2015: 462–476.

2016). Old Kingdom inscriptions in the well-inscribed landscape of Sinai further assert Egyptian royal domination (Bestock, 2018).

Old Kingdom Egyptian administrators in Lower Nubia (O'Connor, 2014) and in the region of Dakhla Oasis governed the areas as occupied foreign territories. Economic activities in those regions suggest a slow move toward integration of Lower Nubia into the larger Egyptian state. Dakhla Oasis became the main center of Old Kingdom power in the Western Desert, with the Early Dynastic Period through the Fourth Dynasty abundantly in evidence at Mut el-Kharab (Hope & Pettman, 2014).

The site of Balat was the base of the governors of Dakhla by the time of the Sixth Dynasty (Pantalacci, 2013a), home to a governor's palace from the reign of Pepi II (ca. 2278–2184 BCE) and a necropolis with large mastabas (Jeuthe, 2018). The palatial architecture and decorated tombs demonstrate the ability of oasis governors to recreate an Egyptian urban landscape far removed from the royal residence (Moeller, 2016: 175–182). Desert patrols monitored the outskirts of the Egyptian settlements in Dakhla, and textual and archaeological sources illustrate interactions, both hostile and pacific, between Egyptians and groups indigenous to the oasis region (Pantalacci, 2013b; Hope, Pettman, & Warfe, 2019). The main route between the Nile Valley and Dakhla was apparently the Darb et-Tawil, with its Nilotic terminus near Asyut. Expeditions from Dakhla explored regions to the southwest, along the Abu Ballas Trail (Förster, 2015).

Titles of officials engaged in desert activities during the late Old Kingdom reveal a decrease in direct royal control over expeditions and a rise in the visible importance of Nubians in the oversight of the desert hinterlands (Diego Espinel, 2014; Raue, 2019). This decentralization of desert oversight appears to have occurred during the reign of the Sixth Dynasty king Merenre (ca. 2287–2278 BCE), when the title "sealer of the god" cedes prominence in desert bureaucracy to officials known as "overseers of Egyptianized Nubians" (*imy-r iꜥ3.w*), with royal oversight continuing in the person of the "royal messenger" (*wpwty-nswt*) (Darnell, 2013b: 788–789). This bipartite administration of desert activity would continue through the New Kingdom.

2.3 The Deserts during the First Intermediate Period and Early Middle Kingdom (ca. 2160–1870 BCE): Incorporation of the Outer Regions

During the late Old Kingdom, governors in the northern portion of the Qena Bend adopted titles consistent with control over the desert hinterlands of Upper Egypt. Trade and mineral resources that flowed through the Wadi Hammamat granted power and wealth to leaders of Coptos in particular (Moreno Garcia, 2017: 100). Only Thebes, however, relatively insignificant during the Old Kingdom, could directly control roads into both the Eastern and Western Deserts. The geopolitical advantages of the city's location contributed to the rise of Thebes during the First Intermediate Period (ca. 2160–2055 BCE), a time of warring southern districts and weak northern kings, based at the city of Heracleopolis.

Control of the desert filling the Qena Bend was of strategic significance, as Theban governors began to move against the Heracleopolitan power and its southernmost bulwark of Coptos. In response to an opposing governor taking control of the Western Desert hinterland of Coptos, the governor of the Coptite district, Tjauti, improved an earlier Western Desert road (Figure 5). A rock inscription on that route, the Wadi Alamat Road, references how the "ruler of another nome" – perhaps a circumlocution for the Theban governor – had annexed, "sealed," the escarpment (Darnell, et al., 2002: 30–46; Mostafa, 2014). By the reign of Theban king Antef II (ca. 2112–2063 BCE), the rulers of Antef's Eleventy Dynasty had extended their control over the entire Qena Bend. Positioned to control the Wadi Hammamat road – shortest road between the Upper Egyptian Nile Valley and the Red Sea – and the Girga Road – shortest

Figure 5 Wadi Alamat Road ascending the escarpment at Gebel Tjauti; inset: the road building inscription of the Coptite governor Tjauti (a white mark indicates the location of the inscription on the rock shelf)

route between the Nile Valley and the southern oases – Thebes emerged triumphant from the wars of the southern governors.

Consistent with annexation of the desert hinterland, the First Intermediate Period Theban general Djemi claims to have "subjected Lower Nubians to *b3k*-status for each governor who arose in this nome"; the *b3k*-status references tax labor, expected of Egyptians and foreigners integrated into the Egyptian economy. King Antef II forged military and political alliances with Nubia (Wegner, 2017/2018), and at roughly the same time, other sources describe desert dwellers bringing *inw*-tribute (Clère & Vandier, 1948: 15, §20).

This situation changed with Montuhotep II (ca. 2055–2004 BCE), during whose reign Lower Nubia and the oases transitioned from occupied outer regions into integrated and regularly tax-paying elements of the Upper Egyptian state (Darnell, 2008; Marochetti 2010: 135, fig. 27b). Montuhotep II established Theban control of all of the Egyptian Nile Valley, ushering in the Middle Kingdom, and annexed Lower Nubia and the southern oases to the Upper Egyptian administration (Darnell, 2013b: 792–793). The great rock inscription of Montuhotep II at the mouth of the Wadi Schatt er-Rigal (see Section 3.9), the terminus of a branch of the Darb el-Gallaba desert road, is further evidence of the importance of desert roads in integrating the oases and the Nubian deserts into the burgeoning Middle Kingdom state. Already before the end of his reign, Montuhotep may also have installed a governor in Dakhla Oasis (Hope & Kaper, 2010).

To assist in administering these newly incorporated outer areas Montuhotep II employed *rwḏw*-agents (probably corresponding to the later *rwḏw ḥq3*, "agent of the ruler"), who combined economic and military responsibilities and resided where they exercised authority. Archaeological evidence for the immediate implementation of Montuhotep II's plan survives in the oasis of Kurkur, where a small structure may represent the official seat of such an agent. The square dry-stone construction (5 m x 5 m), surrounded by C-Group Nubian and early Middle Kingdom ceramic material (roughly at a ratio of 2:1), in an area of circular Nubian huts and tent bases, would be a modest but unmistakable statement of Egyptian presence in the midst of an expansive Nubian settlement.

The burgeoning Middle Kingdom was interested in the human population of desert regions (Darnell, 2004a: 23–37), as well as the trade products of the areas, however modest they may have been. Rock inscriptions in the area of Abisko, of a Nubian soldier named Tjehemau, attest to Montuhotep II's personal recruitment of Nubian auxiliaries in the area (Darnell, 2004a). An inscription of Montuhotep II from the region of Gebel Uweinat in the far southwest (Clayton, de Trafford, & Borda, 2008; Förster, 2015: 479–487), mentioning two otherwise unknown toponyms and depicting them as bringers of tribute, suggests that the founder of the Middle Kingdom may have gone farther than his predecessors in extending the direct influence of the Egyptian state in the southern deserts.

Following a period of internal conflict during the middle portion of the reign of Amenemhat I, the reinvigorated pharaonic state of the Twelfth Dynasty established a physical infrastructure for supporting pharaonic hegemony in the deserts of Egypt and Nubia. The Middle Kingdom continued to exploit the mineral resources of the Eastern Desert and the Sinai Peninsula, and created a base for maritime expeditions to Punt at the Red Sea harbor of Mersa Gawasis (Bard & Fattovich, 2018). At least one expedition of the Middle Kingdom may have stopped at the site of Berenike (Kaper, 2015), which would become a significant Red Sea harbor during the Graeco-Roman Period (see Section 2.7).

Expanding upon the plans of Montuhotep II, Twelfth Dynasty rulers oversaw the construction of a sprawling and complex network of fortresses, towers, and walls along the Second Cataract in Nubia (Vogel, 2004; Kemp, 2006: 231–235; Monnier, 2010: 118–159; Knoblauch, 2019). The Nubian fortresses in the south complemented more modest border outposts on the edges of the eastern (Quirke, 1989; Monnier, 2010: 77–78) and western (Fakhry, 1940) Nile Delta. Although constructed near the margin of the narrow Nubian Nile Valley, Senwosret I's network of Nubian fortresses had as one of its purposes the protection of major desert roads.

Five of Senwosret I's seven major fortifications were situated to guard approaches to mining regions and caravan routes: a drystone fort overlooked the Wadi el-Hudi amethyst mines; settlements at Aniba and Areika monitored the road from Toshka to the carnelian mines and anorthosite gneiss quarries; Ikkur sat opposite the re-envisioned Qubban at the mouth of the Wadi Allaqi, which accessed rich gold mines. This group of fortifications, each a cog in a great machine of border control, projected Egyptian authority over the processing of raw material and goods at nodes of contact with native Nubians, and ensured Egyptian oversight of the provisioning of expeditions and the movement of goods and services from the Nubian deserts into Egypt (Gratien, 2004). The day-book of a scribe based at the fortress of Semna West, found in a late Middle Kingdom tomb on the west bank of Thebes, demonstrates the importance of desert patrols operating out of the Second Cataract fortresses, and the careful surveillance of Egypt's southern border (Smither, 1945; Kraemer & Lizka, 2016).

During the Middle Kingdom, traffic on the desert roads appears to have concentrated on a smaller number of correspondingly more heavily used routes. A police presence is in evidence, in the form of personal names with titles, and even the occasional depiction of a patrolman, at inscription sites (Darnell, et al.,

2002: 56–65, 70, 73–74, 123–124, 137–138, 141, and 143; Darnell, 2002b: 145). The administration of Middle Kingdom Egypt also established patrol routes and smaller installations in the Western Desert, apparently bases of perambulating patrols monitoring traffic on the desert roads (Darnell, D., 2002: 172; Darnell & Manassa, 2007: 85–89, 96). The remains of a consistent pottery kit accompanying most of the assemblages of dry-stone, early Middle Kingdom hut bases on the Theban branches of the Girga Road are physical evidence of official management.

Middle Kingdom Dakhla, former base of Old Kingdom Egyptian control in the west, continued to oversee activities in the hinterlands of that distant oasis (Förster, 2015: 269–276), and Bahariya as well took part in the increased desert traffic of the time (Castel & Tallet, 2001). An additional focus of Middle Kingdom desert activity was the development of the Girga Road between the Nile Valley and Kharga Oasis. Providing some of the best physical evidence for the early Twelfth Dynasty's increased efforts to realize Montuhotep II's plan to attach the southern oases to Upper Egypt is a site now known as Abu Ziyar, located approximately one third of the way out from the Nile Valley on the Girga Road (Darnell & Darnell, 2013). The remains of hundreds of storage jars around a rectangular dry-stone structure – along with other ceramic remains, sigillographic material, and a ^{14}C date – indicate provisioning from the royal residence at Itjy-Tawy during the early Twelfth Dynasty (ca. 1985–1911 BCE). The one administrative unit appearing in the sealings from Abu Ziyar is the treasury, the institution most consistently present in the directorship of mining expeditions. A small ostracon references a group of probably 300 men, under the command of a work foreman (*ṯsw*), a crew probably dispatched by the Nilotic administration to provision the site, on a road previously traveled and now more fully patrolled.

2.4 The Late Middle Kingdom and Second Intermediate Period (1870–1550 BCE) in the Deserts: Bipartite Administration and an Urban Population in the Southern Oases

The Middle Kingdom's efforts to incorporate the oases into the Egyptian state correspond to increased governmental oversight of desert expeditions. Eleventh Dynasty expeditions into the Nubian deserts appear to have been collaborative enterprises between local desert dwellers and Egyptians, the latter including relatively few administrators, chief of whom was an "overseer of Egyptianized Nubians" (Darnell, 2013b: 799–800). During the Twelfth Dynasty, at least some desert missions were larger, with a more complex administration.

By the late Middle Kingdom reign of Amenemhat III (ca. 1831–1786 BCE), a time of particularly intensive mining and quarrying activities in the deserts of Egypt, Nubia, and Sinai,[10] a bipartite system of oversight was in place for desert expeditions. Stelae from the Nubian Gebel el-Asr quarries (for their religious significance, see Section 3.8) indicate that Late Middle Kingdom expeditions were under a dual command, one official reporting along normal lines of established command ("interior overseer of the treasury"), the other having a direct royal appointment ("trustworthy seal bearer"), and both being originally treasury officials (Darnell & Manassa, 2013). Such a system of dual reporting finds later parallels in a stela of the reign of Tutankhamun, from the desert southwest of Aswan (see Section 2.5).

The goal of the early Middle Kingdom travelers and work crews stopping at Abu Ziyar would initially have been Kharga Oasis, even if they were continuing on to the well-established site of Balat in Dakhla Oasis. During the late Middle Kingdom and Second Intermediate Period (ca. 1750–1550 BCE), two hubs of activity developed in Kharga and Dakhla Oases, respectively: the sites of Umm Mawagir and Ain Asil, which flourished when the Thirteenth through Seventeenth Dynasties ruled in the Nile Valley (Darnell & Darnell, 2019).

The two sites share several characteristics. At Umm Mawagir in Kharga Oasis, excavated portions of the settlement indicate that grain processing and baking was taking place there on an industrial scale, in excess of normal household production (Darnell & Darnell, 2016; Darnell & Darnell, 2019). The excavated portion of Umm Mawagir's 'sister-city' of Ain Asil in Dakhla Oasis reveals dozens of silos (Marchand & Soukiassian, 2010), suggesting that Ain Asil may have served a similar supply depot function as that of Umm Mawagir. In the light of the specializations of the Second Cataract fortresses of Twelfth Dynasty date, in which the southern fortress of Askut became a major supply depot (Kemp, 2006: 236–41), Umm Mawagir – the oldest major urban site thus far known in Kharga Oasis – may represent part of an as yet to be fully uncovered network of Middle Kingdom settlements in that oasis.

A small percentage of the population at both Umm Mawagir and Ain Asil consisted of Nubians who maintained contact with Nilotic Nubian groups throughout the late Middle Kingdom and Second Intermediate Period floruits of the sites. The Nubian material at the sites shows affinities to both the Kerma and Pan-Grave cultures (Darnell & Darnell, 2016: 62; also Le Provost

---

[10] Tallet, 2016/2017; González-Tablas Nieto, 2014. The Eastern Desert galena mines at Gebel Zeit continued in use from the late Middle Kingdom through the New Kingdom, and a group of stelae mentioning royal names of the Thirteenth through Seventeenth Dynasties is of historical significance (Régen & Soukiassian, 2008; Marée, 2009).

2016).[11] As at the Nubian fortress of Askut (Smith, 2003), ceramic remains offer insights into parallel Egyptian and Nubian foodways.

Pottery from the two sites in Dakhla and Kharga indicates cultural affiliations with Upper Egypt existing alongside oasis traditions. Egyptian families that had lived in the oases for generations might have fostered a hybrid culture – even identity – much as some Egyptians who garrisoned the fortress of Buhen revealed allegiance to the ruler of Kush during the Second Intermediate Period (Kubisch, 2008: 86–88, 166–78). Without the discovery and analysis of archaeological remains at Umm Mawagir and Ain Asil, the existence of such a culturally complex population in the southern oases during the late Middle Kingdom and Second Intermediate Period might have remained a mystery.

The Umm Mawagir and Ain Asil settlements appear to have been abandoned for other sites in the oases around 1550 BCE.[12] At the same time, the desert roads connecting the Nile Valley and the western oases assumed a new prominence. During the Seventeenth Dynasty, Thebes established an outpost on the Girga Road, halfway between Kharga and the Nile Valley, at a site now called Tundaba after the tundub trees (*Capparis decidua*) that once grew there in some numbers. The small garrison that manned the site from two dry-stone structures could have monitored traffic along the Girga Road, overseeing the large cistern that supplied water to the outpost and any military patrols or trading caravans that passed along the road (see Section 1.4).

The cistern at Tundaba appears to have been an officially controlled water source, the ceramic remains at the site revealing not a push out from the Nile, but rather an interaction at the site of caravans originating almost equally in the Nile Valley and the oases (Darnell & Darnell, 2013: 251–56). An early Eighteenth Dynasty ostracon from one of the dry-stone structures appears to record the calculation of a well tax (Darnell & Darnell, 2013: 250–51). The Tundaba ostracon suggests that the Seventeenth Dynasty and New Kingdom provisioning outposts had become economic entities in their own rights.

Seventeenth Dynasty (Theban) control of the Upper Egyptian Western desert roads provided a strategic check on the power of the Fifteenth Dynasty (Hyksos, centered in the Delta and Middle Egypt) and the kingdom of Kush (a Nubian empire whose capitol, Kerma, was near the Third Cataract). On a stela, the Theban ruler Kamose (ca. 1555–1550 BCE) states (for hieroglyphic text, see

---

[11] Re-examinations of the traditional association of 'Pan Grave' burials and artifacts with the people that the Egyptians call *Mḏꜣy* stress a more nuanced approach (Cooper & Barnard, 2017; Lizka, 2015).

[12] In addition to scattered ceramic remains of Seventeenth Dynasty date at Umm Mawagir and Ain Asil, necropoleis in Dakhla (Hope, 1980: 287–88; 1983: 142–44) and Kharga (see Darnell & Darnell, 2019: 173–74) attest to the oases' inhabitants in that period.

Habachi, 1982: 39, 41): "I captured his [the Hyksos ruler's] messenger in the high desert of the oasis region, while he was traveling south to Kush with a letter." Later in the stela, the episode with the messenger is said to have taken place "on the road." The Girga Road is a plausible candidate for the road in the high desert of the oasis region to which Kamose refers, and an outpost like Tundaba would be a likely base for a patrol that apprehended the Hyksos messenger. In the captured missive, Apepi complains of not being informed about the accession of the new king of Kush, which further supports a model of Theban domination of the Western Desert road network. The Hyksos might have attempted to expand their own territory westwards, using desert roads from Middle Egypt to reach Bahariya Oasis (Colin, 2005). After his forces captured the Hyksos messenger along the oasis road, Kamose dispatched troops to Bahariya, either to attack an existing Hyksos outpost or to prevent the Hyksos from using the oasis as a back-door into Theban territory.

The Seventeenth Dynasty also exploited road networks across the Qena Bend and the Wadi Hammamat road, connecting Coptos with the Red Sea (Polz, 2018: 220–222). Nubkheperre Antef, who built at Coptos and Abydos, appears to have constructed a modest chapel at the Theban terminus of the Farshut Road, overlooking what would become the Valley of the Kings (Polz, 2018: 220–227; Darnell & Darnell, 2019: 178–79). At the southeastern terminus of the Wadi Alamat Road, northwest of Thebes – apparently on the border of the Fourth and Fifth Districts – the Second Intermediate Period Thebans erected two towers, of a roughly cylindrical form, representing a type of defensive construction that persisted virtually unchanged from at least the Early Dynastic Period through the early modern period (Darnell & Darnell, 2019). Control of desert roads leading out of Thebes allowed the Seventeenth Dynasty to bypass sites along the Qena Bend of the Nile, giving Theban patrols access to the Girga Road and Kharga Oasis, and maintaining at least limited access to the mining regions of the Eastern Desert. Ceramic evidence at the Wadi Alamat towers suggests that Nubians as well as Egyptians were stationed at the towers, in keeping with the involvement of Nubian soldiers in Egyptian desert policies from the Old Kingdom onwards.

2.5 Desert Activities during the New Kingdom (ca. 1550–1069 BCE): Expanding Horizons and the Importance of the King's Son of Kush

During the New Kingdom, the southern deserts came under the centralized authority of the Egyptian administration in Nubia. Oversight of military activities to the south, and of pharaonic mining activities in the deserts of Nubia and southern Egypt (Hikade, 2001), became a major responsibility of the King's Son of Kush (*s3 nswt ni Kš*), an office that was itself a creation of the early Eighteenth Dynasty. The Western Desert oases and the routes that connected those regions to the Nile Valley reveal a continued association with Upper Egyptian officials. Egyptian administrators of the oasis region are attested, including bearers of the title "governor of the oasis," sometimes specified as the southern oasis (Kharga and Dakhla) or the northern oasis (Bahariya) (Giddy, 1987: 81–83).

An interconnected oasis ring ultimately linked the Western Desert oases to both the Theban and Memphite centers of power, allowing the Egyptian state to incorporate the Western Desert regions of Egypt and Nubia into a much broader economic sphere. Officials centered in Thebes or Abydos might also have had authority over areas of the Western Desert (Boozer, 2015: 18–19; Bryan, 2006: 100, 104; Giddy, 1987: 82–83; Rossi & Ikram, 2014), and by the reign of Thutmose III (ca. 1479–1425 BCE), the official Puyemre received products from Bahariya and the southern oases as royal donations to the temple of Amun at Thebes (Giddy, 1987: 70), activities suggesting a north to south flow of goods through the oasis ring of the Western Desert.

During the New Kingdom, archaeological sources in the oases and representations in Nilotic tombs illustrate the chief products of the oasis regions. Oasis wine was popular from the Eighteenth through Twentieth Dynasties (Marchand & Tallet, 1999), vintages from the Western Desert being consumed during the jubilee of Amunhotep III (Hope, 2002: 102). Dockets on amphorae from the jubilee city of Malqata (western Thebes) mention *Pr-wsḥ*, the ancient name for Gebel Ghueita in Kharga Oasis.

As in earlier periods of Egyptian history, Egyptianized foreigners were active agents of New Kingdom desert policies, with men such as the royal butler Ramessesemperre acting as a direct representative of Ramesses III (ca. 1184–1153 BCE) at the Timna mines (Sweeney, 2018). A road across the northern Sinai Peninsula, named in ancient Egyptian sources as the "Ways of Horus," provided access to the Egyptian provinces and allies to the northeast, including mineral resources such as the Timna mines (Monnier, 2010: 78–91; Hoffmeier & Moshier, 2013: 487–90; Hoffmeier, 2013).

Medjoy, derived from an earlier designation for a region of Nubia, transformed into a New Kingdom title following the successful employment of Medjoy and other Nubian troops as auxiliaries during the Middle Kingdom and Second Intermediate Period (Liszka, 2010). Captains of Medjoy and their patrolmen were responsible for desert patrols and policing, especially in the Theban necropolises (Vogel, 2015: 438–441). During the New Kingdom fewer titles are associated with the deserts and preserved in rock inscriptions, which may represent to some extent a consolidation of earlier titles and duties (Darnell, 2013b: 819) under the auspices and designation of officers of Medjoy.

During the reign of Thutmose I (ca. 1504–1492 BCE), the military office of commander of Buhen transformed into the truly imperial office of King's Son of Kush, often translated as "Viceroy of Nubia," an attempt to capture how the position was the southern equivalent of the pharaoh in the Egyptian administration of Nubia. Thutmose I also reached beyond the southern border of the Second Cataract, heavily fortified during the Middle Kingdom, apparently incorporated into the Kerma state during the Second Intermediate Period, and recaptured by the late Seventeenth Dynasty. Egypt's newly expanded territory in Nubia stretched as far as Karoy in the south, probably the area of Thutmose I's inscription at Hagar el-Merwa near Kurgus, between the Fourth and Fifth Cataracts (Davies, 2017). By incorporating the Bayuda Desert into the Nubian administration, Thutmose I took control of desert roads that formed the back door to the Second Cataract, firmly establishing the Nubian administration as one focused on both desert and Nilotic routes rather than fortresses (Morris, 2005: 195–199).

In addition to military campaigning and construction activities, one of the chief responsibilities of the King's Son of Kush was the supervision of the tribute of the south, much apparently presented during the great celebrations during which offices were confirmed. Of overweening significance in this wealth of the south was gold mining, an activity under the direct control of the King's Son of Kush. Already under Amunhotep III (ca. 1390–1352 BCE), the King's Son of Kush Merymose adopted the title Overseer of the Gold Lands of Amun (Mahfouz, 2005).

Because desert arteries of mining and trade were more important in determining areas of administrative control than theoretical geographic divisions between districts, the King's Son of Kush exercised authority as far north as the area of Elkab (Davies, 1926: pl. 6). Viceregal subordinates are well attested as far north as the gold-mining region of Wadi Barramiya, east of the area of Edfu (see Section 2.6). The King's Son of Kush might endow religious monuments in the Wadi Hilal east of Elkab (Gabolde, 2015: 240, 256 [Huy under Tutankhamun]; Derchain, 1971: 5–7 [Setau under Ramesses II]), revealing a conjunction of religious, economic, and administrative significance of the desert roads that connected often widely separated regions. The viceregal control of desert activity in the Elkab region probably finds an echo in the Twenty-Fifth Dynasty fortress at Nag Abu Eid, south of Edfu (see Section 2.6).

The number of rock inscriptions in the Eastern Desert increases between the reigns of Thutmose II and Tutankhamun, the peak in this epigraphic effusion occurring during the reign of Amunhotep III. The same period sees an increase in viceregal rock inscriptions, and the number of sites at which pharaonic inscriptions appear (Brown, 2015: 310–316). An expanded bureaucracy under the aegis of the King's Son of Kush, including native Nubians, developed during the reign of Amunhotep II (Darnell, 2014: 272–275), and the final form of the highest levels of the administration – the King's Son of Kush, with two lieutenants representing Lower Nubia (Wawat) and Upper Nubia (Kush) – came into being during the reigns of Amunhotep III and Tutankhamun (Klotz & Brown, 2017).

The reign of Tutankhamun (ca. 1336–1327 BCE) saw considerable attention directed to the patrolling of the Nubian desert roads. The viceroys of Amunhotep III and Akhenaten (ca. 1352–1336 BCE) warred with groups threatening the gold mines of the Wadi Allaqi, and Tutankhamun himself may campaigned against hostile forces to the west of the Nile (possibly the group known as Irem) (Darnell & Manassa, 2007: 119–125). A stela of the reign of Tutankhamun from Kurkur Oasis (Figure 6) refers to the "Western Wall of Pharaoh." Although this Eighteenth Dynasty defensive line might suggest an earlier, southern predecessor of the chain of fortresses Ramesses II constructed in the northern portion of the Western Desert (see Section 2.5), no surviving fortifications hint at any considerable architectural embodiment of this wall.

The "Western Wall" on the Tutankhamun stela from Kurkur probably references a line of outposts and patrol routes along the Sinn el-Kaddab Plateau, extending at least as far as Kurkur Oasis in the north (Darnell, 2003). Dry-stone walls and small structures, perhaps augmented by brush and thorn fences (often called *zeriba*, from Arabic), may well have formed part of this defensive ensemble, but the most important elements would have been the soldiers who patrolled Tutankhamun's "Western Wall." More recently, during the late nineteenth century, local Ababde tribesmen garrisoned Kurkur Oasis without leaving evidence of any massive fortifications (Butzer & Hansen, 1968: 334–335). Fortunately, the Tutankhamun stela from Kurkur provides unexpected information as to how such a patrol functioned.

In the stela's lunette, the king offers incense to the ram-headed god Khnum, while below the Deputy of Wawat (Lower Nubia), Penniut, rebukes a Medjoy patrolman "who guides on the Western Wall." According to Penniut, the patrolman did not "come to take the seal," presumably a signet indicative of his status. The Medjoy responds to this criticism with an overview of his daily duties: "How great are they, the four *iteru* of travel which I make daily; five times going up [the mountain], five times going down [the mountain]; so do not let me be replaced by another!" This description of a patrolman's daily routine of four *iteru*, corresponding to approximately 42 kilometers, is in fact a reasonable albeit long distance for

Figure 6 Stela from the reign of Tutankhamun from the Sinn el-Kaddab
between Kurkur and Dunqul oases

a group to cover in a day.[13] A chain of such patrols, based at the small wells and oases of the Nubian deserts, might well form a human wall for pharaonic Nubia. In the text of the Kurkur Oasis stela of Tutankhamun, the Deputy of Wawat, Penniut, appears to reference a "changing of guard" ceremony, in which he handed a seal directly to a Medjoy patrolman. If indeed a patrolman had a direct link with the Deputy of Wawat via a badge of office, then the Kurkur Oasis stela may provide evidence for a dual system of border monitoring, which may echo the similar system of oversight for Middle Kingdom expeditions (see Section 2.4).

---

[13] According to Herodotus VI 116, the Athenian army returned rapidly to Athens from Marathon after defeating the Persian forces, apparently on the same day of their victory, covering approximately the same distance as that of the Kurkur patrolman's daily round. For running in Egyptian military training in the desert, compare the text of Taharqa in Moussa, 1981: ll. 4 and 12–15.

The suggestion of the Kurkur stela of Tutankhamun is that a Nubian patrol-man without a title placing him high in the administration might have an appointment with a high official, such as the Deputy of Wawat, to collect a seal of office. Such an arrangement, with a direct representative of official authority operating in a border region, apparently reporting directly to a high official rather than along a chain of command, may find a parallel in the Roman *beneficiarius consularis*. Those officials, military veterans who oversaw the functions of border outposts, particularly military roads, reported directly to the cognizant local governors, providing a view of border situations parallel to that of the normal chains of military and bureaucratic command (Darnell, 2003: 81–82).

Some New Kingdom desert tracks appear to have been monitored by mounted patrols, capable of covering even greater daily distances than the Medjoy of the Kurkur Oasis stela (Darnell, et al., 2002: 143–144, 152 n. 8). At the Wadi el-Hol – an important caravan stop with extensive rock art and rock inscriptions on the Farshut Road, located roughly in the middle of the Qena Bend – a late Nineteenth Dynasty stable master left his name, and by the Twenty-First Dynasty, the Farshut Road was known as the "Road of Horses" (Darnell, et al., 2002: 139; Darnell, 2002b: 132–135). Mounted couriers may have functioned like an ancient pony express. Centuries later, Diodorus Siculus (Bk. I, Ch. 45.7) states that in pharaonic times one hundred horse relay posts were strung out between Memphis in the north and the "Libyan mountains" of western Thebes to the south. A letter carried across the Farshut Road from Thebes to Hou, either on foot or on horseback, may in fact survive. P. Berlin 10463 is a brief, hieratic letter sent by Sennefer, mayor of Thebes under Amunhotep II (ca. 1427–1400 BCE), to the farmer Baki of Hou, near modern Farshut (Caminos, 1963a: 32). The letter announces a visit that will occur in three days, suggesting that Sennefer gave his note into the hand of a courier who would have traveled by land, a shortcut across the Qena Bend.

On the Farshut Road, archaeological remains at the Gebel Roma caravansary, on the high plateau above the Wadi el-Hol rock inscription site, may provide evidence for a hoarding economy during the late New Kingdom, which com-plements contemporaneous Nilotic sources describing internal unrest. Extensive stratified deposits of ceramic material, animal dung, and botanical remains formed at the caravansaries (Cappers, Sikking, Darnell, & Darnell, 2007; Darnell, 2007: 43–46). Analysis of botanical material from the late New Kingdom levels shows that the grains in those deposits are undigested, indicat-ing that they were not primarily animal fodder, but most probably destined for Thebes. The Gebel Roma caravansary suggests that officially outfitted caravans transported large amounts of grain – seemingly into the great magazines of the estate of Amun at Thebes – even as famine and civil war rocked late Ramesside Egypt (Darnell, et al., 2002: 154).

Officials involved in the accounting of grain and the oversight of official weights are attested in the rock inscriptions in the Wadi el-Hol. With the name of the second prophet of Amun of Karnak, Roma-Roy – later to become high priest of Amun of Karnak – inscribed on a boulder at the Gebel Roma caravan deposit, these inscriptions support the possibility of a customs center or at least routine checks at the caravansaries on the Farshut Road (Darnell, et al., 2002: 92, 155, 159–160). Even high officials might take personal charge of a grain shipment by boat (Janssen, 2004: 34–36, 66–67), and the material at Gebel Roma and in the Wadi el-Hol provides tangible evidence for this practice for land transport as well.

At a time when the oases were producing desirable wine, the Libyan tribes who inhabited the Eastern Sahara became an increasingly serious threat. The New Kingdom represents a fundamental transformation in the interaction between the Egyptian state and peoples inhabiting the Sahara Desert. Nubian and Libyan auxiliary troops appear in the royal bodyguard of Akhenaton and in processions of military personnel depicted in the Opet Processions scenes of Tutankhamun in the Colonnade Hall of Luxor Temple (Darnell & Manassa, 2007; Darnell, 2010b). Both Libyan and Nubian participants revealed the universality of New Kingdom pharaonic power, and at the same time served to represent the peoples of the southern deserts in festivals associated with the return of the distant goddess (see Section 3.4). Already by the time of Akhenaton, however, we have evidence for conflict involving Egyptians, Libyans, and probably Mycenaeans (or Sea Peoples wearing helmets of Mycenaean style) (Parkinson & Schofield, 1995).

Libya's rise to prominence in the late second millennium BCE emphasizes the overall significance of caravan routes of the Western Desert. Mersa Matruh/ Bates Island is a late Bronze Age harbor and trading depot with connections to the wider Mediterranean world, as abundant imported ceramics indicate (Hulin, 2015). Libyans could trade the wealth of caravans traveling the Eastern Sahara routes with both Egyptian and Mediterranean merchants, and the later highly coveted medicinal plant silphium may have already played an economic role at this early date (Richardson, 1999).

Threats to the western Delta from Libyan groups became increasingly apparent during the Eighteenth and Nineteenth Dynasties. Ramesses II constructed a fortress at Zawiyet Umm el-Rakham to control the northwestern desert road passing between the coast of the Mediterranean and the Qattara Depression, connecting Egypt with Libya proper (Morris, 2005: 621–645; Snape, 2003: 98–105; Snape & Wilson, 2007). Zawiyet Umm el-Rakham was key to guarding the main water sources in the region, and denial of those wells to invading Libyan armies, apparently migrating with both families and livestock, was a key element of Egyptian strategy (Snape, 2013: 447–448). The fortress at Zawiyet Umm el-Rakham was particularly effective, because it could be supplied from transport ships rather than relying on overland routes (Snape, 2013: 450–452).

Nineteenth Dynasty textual sources mention "fortresses" on the Libyan marches of the northern Western Desert, although the identification of sites with the presumed series of fortresses remains difficult (Monnier, 2010: 106–116; Snape, 2013); like Zawiyet Umm el-Rakham, these fortresses would have served as trading centers as much as military bases (Moreno Garcia, 2018: 171–173). By the reign of Merneptah (ca. 1213–1203 BCE), these threats appear in a more sinister and ominous form, as a coalition of Libyans and Sea Peoples used routes between Farafra Oasis and the Nile Valley to mount an invasion of the western Delta (Manassa, 2003). In spite of Merneptah's success in defeating the Libyan threat, numerous Libyan groups appear to have settled in Lower Egypt. Ramesside Egypt ultimately appears to have been unable to stop entirely the raids of Libyan desert "pirates," who made life difficult for those in the Nile Valley, particularly in Late Ramesside Thebes.[14]

2.6 Desert Activities during the First Millennium BCE: Expansion of the Oasis Ring Road

During the reign of the Twenty-First Dynasty high priest of Amun, Menkheperre, the southern administration sought to neutralize criminal elements in the perhaps lawless western oases. Just as Montuhotep II and his immediate successors had earlier exerted control over the oases following a period of reduced administrative control, so Menkheperre attempted through the pardoning oracle of Amun to reconcile the Nilotic government with exiles and others who peopled the oases. Stelae on the Farshut Road, connecting Thebes with the Girga Road and the ring of western oases, fortresses at the Nilotic termini of several desert routes, and inscriptions in the Wadi Hammamat, bear witness to the energy of Menkheperre in reopening the Western Desert to Theban endeavors (Lull, 2006: 227–240; Klotz, 2013: 901–902).

The Nubia-based Twenty-Fifth Dynasty appears to have maintained the Twenty-First Dynasty's focus on fortified control of desert roads by extending a version of the Second Cataract fortresses in Nubia north into Upper Egypt, constructing a major fortification atop a desert crag on the east bank of the Nile

---

[14] See Moreno Garcia, 2018: 159–160; Darnell, 2007: 45–46; Darnell, 2002b: 132–136.

south of Edfu, at a site now called Nag Abu Eid (Aston, 1996). The Twenty-Fifth Dynasty also expanded control of the desert hinterlands of Nubia as well, constructing – or perhaps expanding – a fortress far to the southwest in the Wadi Howar (Jesse, 2019).

Twenty-Sixth Dynasty (664–525 BCE) rulers maintained a series of fortresses in northwestern Sinai, successors to some of the fortresses that guarded the earlier Ramesside "Way of Horus," looking east toward the threat of Persia (Hussein & Alim, 2015). The Persian state would later occupy and augment that string of fortresses. The Saite Period also witnessed considerable exploitation of the greywacke quarries in the Wadi Hammamat (Figure 7), and an expedition appears to have taken the same track between Coptos and the Red Sea, en route to Punt (Betro, 1996).

With the rulers of the first Persian Period in Egypt (the Twenty-Seventh Dynasty, 525–404 BCE), we again see considerable resources devoted to the development and exploitation of the Egyptian deserts. In the Eastern Desert, the Persian rulers of Egypt continued to exploit the mineral wealth of the Wadi Hammamat, with a statue of Darius I at Susa deriving from those quarries (Yoyotte, 2010). Darius I also connected the Nile, and ultimately the Mediterranean, with the Red Sea via a canal in the area of Suez (Klotz, 2015).

Figure 7 Rock inscription of the Twenty-Sixth Dynasty pharaoh Amasis (Ahmose) worshipping the god Min of Coptos (photo by J.-G. Olette-Pelletier)

The Persian Period saw increased activity in the Western Desert, beyond the already energetic Saite attention.[15] Throughout pharaonic history, temples are nodes of economic activity, and Persian temple construction in Kharga Oasis coincides with the introduction of underground aqueducts, the *qanat* irrigation systems, that allowed greater agricultural development of the oases (Newton, et al., 2013). Even during the time of Egyptian independence between the first and second periods of Persian domination, the Twenty-Eighth through Thirtieth Dynasties (404–343 BCE), activity in the oases continued, particularly at Hibis in Kharga Oasis, and farther out at Bahrein and Siwa Oases (Klotz, 2013: 907–908).

Under the energetic attention of the early Achaemenid rulers of the Twenty-Seventh Dynasty, the disparate oases of the Egyptian Western Desert became an integrated network, an archipelago of trade entrepots linking Egypt and Nubia with Cyrenaica and points beyond. Even as late as the time of the final pre-Ptolemaic dynasties, an administrator could combine broad duties in Upper Egypt with oversight in the oases (Darnell 2013b, 818). When Alexander the Great wrested Egypt from Persian control in 332 BCE, he visited the temple of Amun in Siwa Oasis, both establishing himself as the son of Amun and proper pharaoh, and asserting a desire to continue what may have been already the Persian drive to extend into Cyrenaica and perhaps beyond into the Carthaginian realm (Müller, 2016). Eventually, with the marriage of Ptolemy III to the princess Berenike of Cyrene, the apparent Persian Period Egyptian goal of control of Cyrenaica was accomplished.

Ptolemaic rulers continued both the building program of their predecessors in the Western Desert oases and the economic integration of those areas with the Nile Valley (Gill, 2016). Three short inscriptions of Persian Period and Ptolemaic date at Ghueita Temple, in Kharga Oasis, demonstrate how temple economies created far-reaching connections with points in the Nile Valley, and others farther north and west in the Western Desert (Darnell, et al., 2013). In a bandeau inscription of the sanctuary of Ghueita Temple and in a parallel text on the exterior of Hibis Temple, Darius I refers to the importation of "coniferous wood of the Western Desert." These texts are epigraphic evidence for the importation of cedar (or perhaps juniper) from the west into Kharga Oasis, and suggest a desire by Darius I to connect Egypt to the trade of Cyrenaica via the oases of the Western Desert.[16] Kharga would then be a link in a chain of oases stretching west and northwest to Kufra, Augila, and even beyond.

---

[15] See Klotz, 2013: 906–907; Boozer, 2015: 21–25 (and references therein); Hubschmann, 2019.

[16] Liverani, 2000: 512–513; compare Herodotus, *Histories*, III 17; for the question of North African coniferous wood in ancient Egypt (although he is not aware of the Ghueita text), see Bardinet 2008.

A bandeau text of Ptolemy III within the hypostyle hall of Ghueita Temple states that building activities at the site were carried out "in order to direct divine offerings to Thebes," perhaps a reference to the agricultural products of Kharga Oasis. In additional bandeau texts in the same hypostyle hall, both Ptolemy III and Ptolemy IV claim to provision Ghueita Temple with "all good things of Bahariya Oasis." Together these inscriptions reveal the importation of products from Bahariya Oasis to Ghueita in Kharga Oasis. The export of Ghueita's bounty – perhaps including some if not all of her Bahariyan imports – to Thebes demonstrates the importance of Gebel Ghueita, and Kharga Oasis as a whole, to commerce in the Western Desert during the Ptolemaic Period. The earlier functioning of an oasis ring road may be supposed; the Twenty-Fifth Dynasty ruler Piye summoned vintners from Bahariya to help with the wines for Amun of Gempaaton, modern Kawa in Sudan (Klotz, 2013: 903), perhaps a way of demonstrating Nubian control of the oasis ring road.

With equal if not greater vigor, the Ptolemaic state exploited the Eastern Desert as well. In addition to continuing in the footsteps of their pharaonic predecessors of three preceding millennia in continuing and even expanding the mining of mineral resources, the Ptolemies continued to pursue the Red Sea interests of the Persian Period rulers (Sidebotham, Hense, & Nouwens, 2008). Initially an interest in procuring elephants for use in the wars of the Diadochoi may have dominated Ptolemaic interests in the Red Sea, but long distance Red Sea and Indian Ocean trade was a major aspect of Eastern Desert activity that the Ptolemies bequeathed to their Roman Period successors (Sidebotham, 2011).

2.7 Roman Egypt and Indigenous Desert Groups (30 BCE – 600 CE)

The Roman Period saw intensification of agriculture in the oases of the Western Desert, and the creation of a line of fortifications, often with associated settlements, in Kharga Oasis during the third and fourth centuries CE (Rossi & Ikram, 2018). The southern oases shared a vibrant culture, independent of the Nilotic world, that appears to have built upon a Ptolemaic base, attaining a particularly Roman-Egyptian character around the middle of the first century CE (Kaper, 2012). Mining and quarry settlements, many with temple complexes, expanded in the Eastern Desert under Roman rule, with fortified wells established along several important roads (Sidebotham & Gates-Foster, 2019; Sidebotham, Hense, & Nouwens 2008: 37–94, 118–143, 213–256). Red Sea trade also appears to have increased during the Roman Period, the southeastern port of Berenike becoming an emporium linking Egypt with the Indian Ocean and points beyond (Sidebotham, 2011), ultimately connecting the Red Sea and Mediterranean worlds with southeast Asia and China (Young, 2001: 32–34).

The later third century CE was a time of considerable turmoil in Egypt, with a resulting drop in Red Sea and Indian Ocean trade. Much of this disruption may result from raids of a desert group known as the Blemmyes, who took control of Coptos from 268 to 270 CE, and the Palmyrene invasion from 270–272 CE. The subsequent war of Diocletian against the usurper Domitius Domitianus sees the destruction of the city of Coptos, Nilotic emporium for most of the southern routes of the Eastern Desert. Following these crises, the fourth century CE witnessed the resumption of activity at the Red Sea ports and elsewhere in the Roman Egyptian deserts (Young, 2001: 80–88; Sidebotham, 2011: 259–282). During this time of resurgent desert trade, we see a new type of settlement appear in the southern Eastern Desert (Figure 8), in spite of continued Blemmye raids, and perhaps even associated with the compatriots of those desert people.

After millennia of the Eastern Desert being primarily a goal of mining and quarrying expeditions, and the region of corridors of long distance trade linking Egypt to the Red Sea, a new type of settlement site appeared in the southern Eastern Desert during the Late Roman Period (ca. 400–600 CE). Dating to a roughly two century period centered on ca. 500 CE, these settlements – frequently termed "Enigmatic Sites" – share a distinctive style of dry-stone architecture, a fairly standardized Late Roman ceramic corpus, and a similar approach to adapting dry-stone architecture to the wadi landscape. Most of the sites are along desert roads, with some of the larger sites associated with smaller, satellite settlements of usually less complex structures. In association

Figure 8 View (from cliff opposite the wadi) of structures at the Late Roman site of Umm Buyut (for location, see Map 5)

with several of these Late Roman sites are cairn tombs and tumuli (Lassányi, 2012: 262–265; Krzywinski, 2012: 152–153).

In terms of number of sites, size and density of structures, and richness of associated archaeological material, these settlements center on the area to the east of Moalla (Darnell & Darnell, 2020; Sidebotham, Barnard, & Pyke, 2002: 189; Sidebotham, Hense, & Nouwens, 2008: 371–375; Vasáros, 2010: 201–202). Unlike campsites or barracks for quarrying and mining, the structures at the desert sites include some large multi-room complexes, and none of the sites reveals any evidence for associated quarrying or mining activities (Lassányi, 2010: 601). Eastern Desert Ware is attested in association with the Enigmatic Sites at Umm Buyut, east of Elkab, and with the Late Roman sites near Moalla. Whether Eastern Desert Ware can be identified as a cultural marker for the Blemmyes, as has been suggested (Edwards, 2004: 208–209), remains a matter of debate (Barnard, 2008).

Most likely, these sites are settlements of indigenous Eastern Desert dwellers (Lassányi, 2012: 253–269; Darnell & Darnell, 2020; unconvincingly rejected in Sidebotham, Barnard, & Pyke, 2002: 222–223). Both the geographical extent and chronological range of the settlements correspond to the general area and time in which Greek and Egyptian documents place a group called the Blemmyes, who exerted some political and economic control over the Eastern Desert. By the end of the third century CE and especially during the fourth and fifth centuries CE, historical and documentary sources provide increasingly specific information about the Blemmyes (Pierce, 2012). One document (P. Köln ägypt. 13) refers to a woman dwelling in either a city or a *komerkion*, the latter a term derived from Latin and meaning a "place for trade." While Gebelein on the Nile would be a traditional city, the rare term *komerkion* may refer to one of the desert settlements, such as Wadi Mahmiyyet ad-Debabiya (M10-11/S1), due east of Gebelein (Darnell & Darnell, 2020).

In Lower Nubia, the Blemmyes prioritized interactions with the Isis Temple at Philae; further to the east, Blemmyes engaged in mining, specifically the extraction of emeralds (the unnamed location is probably Mons Smaragdus: Dijkstra, 2012: 244). Textually attested Blemmye raiding of Nile Valley settlements – at odds with the lives of more settled Blemmyes – may represent attempts to augment the precariously balanced ecology of desert dwelling elements of the Blemmye population. Though profiting from trade and perhaps even overseeing much of it, the desert Blemmyes would have remained subject to occasional shortfalls of both material income and the products of hunting, husbandry, and the occasional and widely scattered cultivation opportunities in the Eastern Desert (Kuznar & Sedlmeyer, 2008). By the end of the sixth century the Blemmyes were an at least partially desert dwelling population, well established in the region of Moalla, a perhaps semi-autonomous and semi-sedentary group owing taxes to the Eastern Empire (Dijkstra, 2012: 246–247; Faraji, 2011; Dijkstra, 2008: 162–163).

A comparison of the monastic economy of the Western Desert, with its diverse architectural manifestations, to the Late Roman sites of the Eastern Desert may offer some insight into the possible functions of the latter. Similar "Enigmatic Sites" do not occur elsewhere in the northern Eastern Desert, nor do they appear in the Western Desert, but they are present in Nilotic Lower Nubia (Krzywinski, 2012: 152–153; Lassányi, 2012: 256–258), also consistent with a Blemmye association. Although such sites are absent in the Western Desert, an architectural phenomenon of similar date and perhaps corresponding function does appear in the desert hinterland of Naqada, Thebes, Armant, and Esna. A number of generally modestly sized monastic settlements appear in the middle and high desert, often well beyond the larger monastic communities generally settled at the very edges of the desert (compare the map in Doresse, 1949: 506).

The deep-desert monasteries of the Theban Western Desert and the Late Roman sites of the southern Eastern Desert may represent similar responses of different but interconnected societies to a similar need – the projection of economic authority into marginal areas. The rise of both approaches to control of the deserts corresponds to a period of diminished efforts of the Nilotic government to administer desert regions. The period of the Enigmatic Settlements in the east and the network of monastic sites in the west also corresponds to the great increase in the use of the camel, and the concomitant social and economic implications thereof.

3 Desert as Numinous Space

The desert could be a sacred landscape for the ancient Egyptians, both as a home to certain deities, and more generally as the stony womb of the blocks and statues that continually embellished and enlarged the temples of Egypt and Nubia. Desert associations with deities might be geographically specific, such as Sopdu as lord of the east (Valbelle & Bonnet, 1996: 38–39), and Min of Coptos (Figure 7) as a god of the Eastern Desert and the roads thereof (Darnell, et al., 2002: 122–123; Darnell, 2013a: 73; Olette-Pelletier, f.c.). In the west, the deity Igay, lord of the oases (Hope & Kaper, 2010: 227–229), and the Libyan divinity Ash (Willeitner, 2003: 146 n. 51) shared the desert expanses with the obscure Ha, divine personification of the Western Desert (Leitz, et al., 2002: 10–11). One deity above all others bore a more conceptual association with the deserts: Seth as god of the Red Land, one of a number of characteristics setting him in opposition to his counterpart, the god Horus as lord of the Black Land. Nevertheless, desert travelers appear most frequently to have invoked Seth in the hinterlands of his main cult sites, such as Naqada and Dakhleh Oasis (Darnell, 2013a: 126–127; Polkowski, 2019).

The deities most prominent at the greatest number of pharaonic desert sites are neither the specific divine manifestations of the Eastern and Western Deserts, nor Seth as representative of the Red Land, but rather Hathor and Horus, the latter deity frequently present in the form of the deified ruler (Darnell & Manassa 2013: 57). Mines and quarries might have their own divinities (Meeks, 1991), including the goddess Hathor, to whom authors of graffiti might address themselves. The reason for the sacred nature of such places, as well as the religious significance of sites such as desert crossroads, is connected with an Egyptian approach to the landscape, one in which the deserts played a vibrant part.

3.1 Being-in-the-Landscape

Especially at the crossroads, junctures, and termini of desert roads, on the surfaces of rocks overlooking the points where the often broad tracks of a road across flat desert would converge at a desert pass – at such places the ancient Egyptians, both those of the pharaonic age and their Predynastic predecessors, were wont to carve images and inscriptions on the desert surface. Rock art and inscription sites represent points of human engagement with the desert landscape, an interaction between humans and desert landforms creating places in the vastness and thereby socializing the desert (Darnell, 2009: 85–87; Riemer & Förster, 2013: 42; Brown, 2017). The ancient Egyptian creators of these inscribed places, and the later visitors who literally wrote their presence into the desert landscape, sought both to memorialize themselves, and to interact with the memorials of their predecessors, resulting in abundant inscriptional evidence of ancient activities in the Eastern and Western Deserts.

The modern epigrapher must reconstruct long vanished conjunctions of artist/writer, concept, iconography/script, and environment that produced each example of ancient rock art and each rock inscription (Lovata, 2015). An anthropological approach to such locations views landscape as an element in human practices (Fowler, 2008; Waterton, 2013), with rock art and inscription sites representing the results of activities – even performances – that structured and interrelated the human body, perception, and the landscape itself (Wylie, 2007: 166). All human senses engage in the personal experience of landscape, through which a human actor may merge with both the event and the landscape (Crouch, 2010: 14). The desert is neither merely a theater of action nor an object of attention, but an element in a sensual encounter between both human and landscape. Graffiti in Egypt interact with man-made "landscapes" of temples and tombs, as well as with the deserts themselves, becoming examples of "performative" texts.[17]

One class of graffiti, carved images of human feet or sandals, is present both in desert rock art (Figure 9) and on the roofs and pavements of temples. These outlines of feet (*vestigia*) represent the visual echoes of such interactions of people, objects, and landscapes, and reveal at least some rock art and rock inscriptions to be vestiges of human actions more than independent visual impositions on objects and places. The outlines of feet appear as rock inscriptions at a number of desert sites (Váhala & Cervicek, 1999: no. 45 *et passim*; Darnell, 2002a: 121; Kaper & Willems, 2002: 85–88; Polkowski, 2018), and are even more prominent in temple graffiti, the outlines often containing the name of the carver, with perhaps filiation (Jacquet-Gordon, 2003). Although some may have the appearance of footprints, or of feet viewed from above, others depict unlaced sandals. Third Intermediate Period texts accompanying some of the foot outlines on the roof of Khonsu Temple at Karnak designate the carvings as *dgs* (Jacquet-Gordon, 2003: 41), a term for "footprint" deriving from the verb *dgs,* "to step," and referencing each image as a record of a body once in motion at the site. At a rock art site in the eastern portion of the Wadi Hilal (east of Elkab) are dozens of Old Kingdom *vestigia* that appear alongside carvings of hands, which are much rarer in rock art (Darnell, in press c). Other items of personal equipment sometimes appear in rock art (Kaper & Willems, 2002: 85, 88), and these may as well serve a similar function to that of the *vestigia* – reflections onto the desert body of human bodies once in motion in the landscape.

For the ancient Egyptians, the landscape through which they moved, and on which they left the visual and textual records of their activities, was an active presence, another body. When the ancient Egyptians engaged with the desert hinterlands of the Nile Valley, they interacted with an entity, a "you" rather than an "it."[18]

3.2 The Desert Landscape as Entity

The Egyptians could identify the minerals and stones of the deserts as concretized exudations of a celestial goddess, who in Pyramid Text Utterance 350

---

[17] Note Plesch, 2015, concerning the performative aspect of graffiti on frescoes in fifteenth century Italian churches; she also observes (p. 53), "It could be argued that graffiti, to varying degrees perhaps, but always to some extent, interact with their support, and that the support is part of the message."

[18] For additional references to this section see Darnell, 2020a.

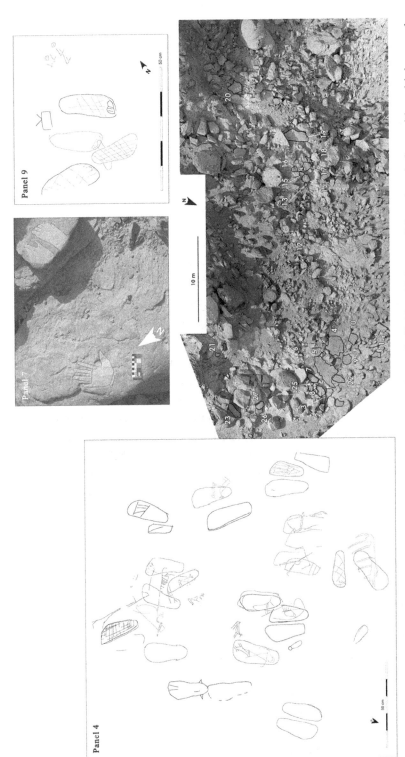

Figure 9 Rock inscription site in the eastern portion of the Wadi Hilal (east of Elkab), with insets of three inscriptions with multiple carved feet and sandal outlines (Panels 4 and 9), and two hands (Panel 7)

"strews greenstone, malachite, turquoise – the stars" (Sethe, 1908: 292–293, §567a-c; Berger-El Naggar, et al., 2010: 196). Mining expeditions, seeking and extracting the mineral glory shed by the goddess, therefore engaged in activities of cosmic significance. An inscription from the reign of Senwosret I (ca. 1990 BCE) in the amethyst quarries in Wadi el-Hudi (Sadek, 1980: 84, ll. 5–9) describes mining activities in an epic mode:

> For him (the ruler) has Geb (the earth god) decreed his hidden things,
>> hill lands presenting, mountains being kind.
> Every place has given what it conceals,
>> his emissaries numerous in all lands,
>> messengers doing what he has desired – that which is in his sight –
>> on coasts and in deserts.
> To him belongs what the sun disk encircles,
>> what the eye brings to him from what is in her,
>> the mistress of transformations from all that she creates.

The cosmic goddess Hathor, "the eye" (of the sun god), yields to the Egyptian ruler the minerals of which she is composed. In essence, the mineral wealth of Egypt's desert hinterlands is consubstantial with the body and bodily emanations of the solar eye goddess. The concept of minerals and stones as concretized effluvia may to some extent explain the occasional reverence toward fossils and natural oddities (Aufrère, 1999b; Welvaert, 2002; von Lieven, 2013).

The landscape can be a divine body, whose functions produce the agricultural and mineralogical bounty of the Egyptian world. The corpse of Osiris, embodying the fertile black soil of the Nile Valley, could emit the Nile as the product of putrefying efflux, and the $\underline{h}$3.t-body of Amun could q3^c-spew forth the Nile, so an open-pit mine – also called $\underline{h}$3.t – could q3^c-spew forth its stones (Darnell, 2020a). A stone cutter could be termed "one who brings a stone to life" ($s^c n \underline{h}$ *inr* – Aufrère, 1991: 78), and a carved stone might in turn bring some aspect of the living desert with it, and be called a "living entity" ($^c n \underline{h}$ – Hannig, 2006: 541; Aufrère, 1991: 100). Cut stones might even join other elements of the cosmos in praising the creator (Aufrère, 2007: 67–77).

As the desert could represent a great cosmic body for the ancient Egyptians, so the surfaces of rocks and minerals share both the qualities and lexicography of human skin. A Middle Kingdom inscription recording the mining of turquoise at Serabit el-Khadim in Sinai (sixth regnal year of Amenemhat III, ca. 1854 BCE) describes turquoise as the very skin of the goddess Hathor. The official Horwerre details the problems inherent in mining the blue-green mineral during the summer, and provides advice to future miners (Gardiner, Peet, & Cerny, 1952: pl. 26; Valbelle & Bonnet, 1996: 14 [fig. 14] and 119–120 [figs. 141-142b]):

Behold – through the green does Hathor reveal herself.
Even as I have seen so have I done the like myself.

I came from Egypt, my face downcast –
Mysterious in my view was the finding of her (Hathor's) true color/skin,
    when the desert burns during the season of Shomou,
    the mountains burning like a brand, the color/skin pale/blistered.

The text describes the pale color of the turquoise in the same way as it might depict the blistering of skin. The Egyptian words for color (*iwn*) and skin (*inm*) can interchange in certain contexts, evoking to the range of meanings of Greek *chroma*, "skin, complexion, embellishment" (Darnell, 2010a: 106–107). Thus Hathor in Sinai may adopt the epithet "lady of the good color/perfect skin" (*nb.t inm nfr*). Even the term for engraving on a stone – *mtn* – can also apply to etching a tattoo into human skin (Darnell, 2018: 403).

Human skin is a surface onto which tattooing or painting can project outer forms, a material onto the surface of which an inherent aspect of the person may manifest itself (Fleming, 2001: 79–112). Other cultures reveal connections between the pigments for bodily adornment and the use of the same pigments in rock art (Taçon, 2004; Robinson, 2004). The malachite applied around the eyes of a Predynastic female statuette (Metropolitan Museum of Art 02.228.71; Patch, 2011: 122–123) provides a direct link between the desert mine and the woman depicted, whose body is also adorned with images of hunting that appear so often in Predynastic rock art.

The surfaces of rocks and human skin can bear representations that prepare both for social activities (Darnell, 2018: 407; compare Rainbird, 2008: 266). Naqada II (ca. 3500–3250 BCE) figurines of women, probably ritualists, can show the human body decorated with imagery in style and concept parallel to that of rock art – hunting scenes, and a blending of Nilotic and desert imagery. These illustrated women foreshadow the use of tattooing to embellish the bodies of later female musicians and ritualists (Poon & Quickenden, 2006). The bodies of some desert hunters, in depictions from a rock art site in the Wadi Nag el-Birka, were also decorated with similar imagery (Darnell, in Hendrickx, et al., 2010: 216–218). The interrelationships of tattoo styles and rock art depictions postulated on the basis of two- and three-dimensional depictions (Darnell, 2018) was confirmed with the identification of the earliest figural tattoos in ancient Egypt (Friedman, et al., 2018). Those tattoos on a naturally mummified late Predynastic man, probably from Gebelein, include a bull and a barbary sheep, images that find their best parallels in the elite hunting imagery of the Predynastic Egyptian rock art corpus. The skins of both desert rocks and human hunters or ritualists could reflect images of human activities that occurred within the desert landscape.

Humans and landscapes could share characteristics (compare Herero and Himba praise poems in Namibia – Bleckmann, 2007), and even visual characters.

3.3 The Desert as Repository of Sacred Objects *in ovo*

Early Egyptian rock art occasionally took advantage of the physical appearance of the rock surface, incorporating boat drawings into natural curving folds of rock (Figure 10), even interacting with cracks in the stone (compare Darnell, 2009: 91; Darnell, 2011: 1155–1156). Such epigraphic responses to natural forms may represent iconographic attempts to reveal concepts or shapes latent within the stone (compare cross-culturally Whitley, 1998; Dowson, 1998). By virtue of the objects resulting from the stones it provided, a mine might be said to produce divine offspring – an inscription of the reign of Montuhotep IV in the Wadi Hammamat refers to a portion of the site as the "divine nest of Horus" (Couyat & Montet, 1912: 98 [no. 192, ll. 4–5]), home for royal works *in ovo*.[19]

Several texts attest to the concept of statues and other objects inhabiting stones before they are carved – sculptures populate even the unexcavated quarry. Miners and sculptors removed covering elements of the stony cortex that shrouded the quarry's natural gifts, freeing them for their proper purpose. Even at the time of a quarry's discovery, stones and images yet to be extracted and inscribed are already present. According to a rock stela of Seti I at Aswan (Habachi, 1973), even as the king identified a new quarry, he perceived the monuments it would yield. Royal perspicacity could even identify elements from different sites that would come together in a single monument – so the text of a formal rock inscription of Seti I from Aswan (Kitchen, 1975: 73, 6–13 [citing ll. 11–12]):

> Then his majesty found a new quarry,
>> containing colossal statues of black granite,
>>> their crowns thereof from the red mountain of the mountain of quartzite.

Latent within the images to be released from the quarry at Aswan, discovered at the same time yet resting in another quarry near Heliopolis, were quartzite crowns. Similarly, the Manshiyet es-Sadr stela of Ramesses II describes how the king created a quarry near Heliopolis, at that red mountain that Seti I foresaw producing the crowns for his statues from Aswan (Kitchen, 1979: 360, 7–362, 12 [citing 361, ll. 8–9]):

> During the same time his majesty found another open quarry near it,
> with (containing) statues of quartzite resembling cedar wood.

---

[19] Compare also the "miraculous" events in the Montuhotep IV inscriptions and the innate power of materials – Nyord, 2020: 29–33.

Figure 10 Rock art and inscription site in the Wadi of the Horus Qa-a; inset: Predynastic carving of a boat with rectangular cabin and multiple oars; the hull is a partially augmented natural feature of the stone

These Nineteenth Dynasty texts make explicit the ancient Egyptian concept that quarries are pre-existing, awaiting discovery, already containing the statuary and blocks that need only the skill of Egyptian miners and artists to release them (Darnell, 2018: 406). The ritual of Opening the Mouth, performed to allow a spiritual force to inhabit a statue or a mummified corpse, describes the similar visualization of a statue within an unworked stone (Fischer-Elfert, 1998).

3.4 Worship in the Desert

With the desert a manifestation of divinity, a sentient being in its own right that delivered into the hands of Egyptian miners and artisans the objects and treasures slumbering within its stones and minerals, the Egyptian deserts were well suited to be places of worship. The sacred nature of the objects to which their stones would contribute, the sacred precincts their stones would build, made of the mines and quarries themselves sacred sites (Darnell, 2020a). A number of quarry areas reveal the presence of both formal religious architecture, and more informal manifestations of worship. The Theban Western Desert and the massif overlooking the west bank of Thebes, in the numerous clefts and wadis of which were nestled the tombs of kings and officials, was a sacred landscape as well (Darnell, 2013a: 75–76; Rummel, 2020). Also on the west bank of Thebes, a high spur of rock to the south of the temple of Montuhotep II provided priests of the early Twelfth Dynasty with a place of desert vigil while looking for the beginning of the Beautiful Festival of the Valley, and the navigation of Amun from Karnak to the west bank (Winlock, 1947: 77–90).

A meaningful perambulation of sacred desert sites is textually attested, particularly during the New Kingdom (Darnell, 2013a: 78) – a worshipper might even be compared to a "jackal of your (the god's) mountains" (Demarée, 2002: pl. 95, l. 2). An unfinished Middle Kingdom tomb at Deir el-Bahari (western Thebes) provides some suggestion of what may have occurred during some of these worshipful walks in the near desert. The tomb, in the cliff to the north of the temples of Montuhotep II, Hatshepsut, and Thutmosis III, was visited, inscribed, and "illuminated" by several New Kingdom visitors (Ragazzoli, 2017). The epigraphic material includes an ink inscription written within the outline of a formal stela, numerous names, and images including a representation of a couple engaged in sexual intercourse.

Thus decorated, the unfinished Deir el-Bahri tomb may have assumed the role of a temporary structure erected for a religious celebration. New Kingdom love poetry attests to such structures, "beer huts," places for drinking and amorous activities (Darnell, 2010a: 129–130). Larger versions of such temporary shrines, formal versions of the "beer huts," are the rock-cut shrines of Gebel Silsilah and Qasr Ibrim (Caminos, 1963b). Although the Gebel Silsilah shrines are located along the west bank of the Nile, they remain desert shrines, cut into the rocks overlooking a stretch of the river entirely lacking in cultivable land. The immediate juxtaposition of Nile and desert at Gebel Silsilah appears to have called to mind for the Egyptians a perpetual state of inundation (compare Bommas 2003).

An important object of worship in the desert was the goddess Hathor, about whom an astronomically based tale of an annual cosmic sojourn arose. As the sun declines into the southern skies during the winter and the season of the low water level of the Nile, so the goddess of the solar eye leaves Re, her father, and Egypt, roaming the southern deserts in her anger. Enticed back to Egypt, by the god Thoth or her brother Onuris-Shu, she eventually returns at the time of the summer solstice and the coming of the Nile inundation. The account in mythic form is known from the Book of the Heavenly Cow, the earliest surviving copies of which date to the New Kingdom, but earlier texts reference the revels that might accompany the goddess's return, and the concept is perhaps much older (Darnell, 2010a).

The late Book of Traversing Eternity references a communal ritual of traveling "upon the desert together with her majesty on the morning of the Menbit festival," the immediate precursor to "going about the region of Asheru when Mut is pacified" (Herbin, 1994: 157–158, 441, pl. 3 [ll. 2–3]). These perambulating events appear to have taken place during the month of Tybi, the returning and yet disquieting goddess of the eye of the sun being escorted by worshippers, who then disport with her in the Mut complex at Karnak in her newly adopted form of the pacified goddess (Bryan, 2014: 103–114). Although the text describing the desert portion of the ritual is of Graeco-Roman Period date, the architectural setting of the "hall of drunkenness" at the Mut complex – the "region of Asheru" – dates to the reign of the Eighteenth Dynasty ruler Hatshepsut (ca. 1473–1458 BCE). A text of Roman Period date at the temple of Medamûd describes such a revel, with Egyptians and foreigners together returning with the far-wandering goddess (Darnell, 1995). Such celebrations would have involved a welcoming of the goddess in the desert, and a return with her to a Nile Valley temple, involving Egyptians and Nubians in the roles of the desert dwelling southern groups with whom the goddess dwelt during the winter. At times, actual representatives of the people from those southern deserts may have taken part in the ritual.

Hierakonpolis Site 64, an isolated rock outcrop with inscriptions at the northwest desert edge of the ancient city, provides rare archaeological evidence of desert ritual activities that linked Nilotic Egyptians and their desert dwelling neighbors. Nubian groups, probably during the Middle Kingdom, utilized the leeward side of the outcrop for campfires (Friedman, 1999: 20–23). An adjacent pit contained a carefully arranged deposit of ostrich feathers and small, inscribed sandstone flake that may reference the goddess Hathor by her epithet "Gold" (Darnell, in press a). In the desert of Hierakonpolis, desert dwellers and Nubians may have joined with Nilotic Egyptians to welcome back the goddess and exchange objects of cultic value, just as the later hymn from Medamûd describes (Darnell, 1999: 27–29). Other rock art depictions in Egypt and Nubia of figures in festal garb or men engaged in ritual combat and wrestling illumin- ate other events that may have coincided with celebrations at desert sites (Darnell, 2013a: 75).

3.5 Rock Inscriptions as Records of Religious Activity

Some rock inscriptions provide evidence for otherwise poorly attested desert rituals (Darnell, 2002a: 112–114). Whereas visitors to religious sites in and near the Nile Valley tended to leave more or less formulaic inscriptions, worshippers at remote desert sites appear more frequently to have felt a freedom to innovate. In spite of their generally informal modes of execution, the visitors' inscriptions at the temples of Deir el-Bahari are for the most part formulaic in wording and content (Pinch, 1993: 356–357). More removed from a major temple, and in a rocky landscape, albeit within the current of the Nile, rock inscriptions on the island of Sahel are conservative, few venturing beyond names and titles (Gasse & Rondot, 2007). These two sites closer to the Nile Valley can be contrasted with the rock inscriptions at the Wadi el-Hol (Darnell, et al., 2002) and the literary and iconographic virtuosity of the priest Pahu, who created his own personal shrine west of Qamula (see Section 3.6).

Nevertheless, even at a desert site amenable to greater innovation, earlier graffiti could exert influence on those who came later. The reproduction of earlier images and inscriptional formulae, even augmentation and updating of earlier carvings, is underway already during the early Predynastic Period. A process of "iconographic attraction" is well attested at a number of Predynastic/Early Dynastic rock inscription sites in the Theban Western Desert, causing specific image types to cluster in particular locations within a much larger site (Darnell, 2009: 93–94). A Middle Kingdom example of similar "attraction" is inscriptions at "Hieroglyph Hill" at Abd el-Qadir, near Serra in Nubia (Hintze & Reineke, 1989: 7–27). The consistency of the inscriptions' content – name, title, dedicatory formula, and associated human figure – suggests that successive visitors intentionally repeated the pattern.

Hellenistic and early Roman Period inscriptions at el-Kanais (55 km east of Edfu) evince an awareness of earlier texts and images, both those in the rock-cut temple and on nearby rock faces (Mairs, 2011). A Graeco-Roman Period inscription at Gebel Silsilah (Preisigke & Spiegelberg, 1915: pl. 20, no. 282, ll. 2–4) indicates that as part of a dialog with the inscription, the reader should raise the hand and perform the ecstatic *gsgs*-dance (Ashby 2018) in the presence of the god Monthu.

Sites such as the Wadi el-Hol demonstrate the creativity and diversity of expression at a major rock inscription site. Several Middle Kingdom visitors to the Wadi el-Hol vividly describe their visit to the site as "spending the day beneath this mountain on holiday" (Darnell, et al., 2002: 129–138). In combination with other inscriptions depicting singers and the goddess in her bovine form (Darnell, et al., 2002: 93–94, 126–132), the "spending the day" inscriptions provide evidence of Hathoric worship in the remote desert, even a deep desert aspect of the Theban "going out upon the desert" that ended in drunken revelry at the temple of Mut. One of the Wadi el-Hol texts includes the detail that the official is there with his coworkers.

Members of the priesthood left inscriptions at a variety of desert sites, some as participants in formal expeditions into the deserts (Seyfried, 1981), and others traveling as part of their religious duties (Darnell, et al., 2002: 95, 102, 120). Textual and archaeological evidence for royal statues in the desert reveals a further facet of priestly presence at rock inscription sites (see Section 3.9).

Old Kingdom rock inscriptions in the Wadi Hilal (east of Elkab) predate surviving temples at the site, but provide information on the functioning and object of the cult (Vandekerckhove & Müller-Wollermann, 2001: 341–342; Darnell, 2004b: 154–155) – a local Elkab New Year celebration of the return of the regional goddess Nekhbet. A close reading of the Wadi Hilal inscriptions combined with new archaeological discoveries even suggests that the large rock that was the main focus of the priests' rock inscriptional activity was itself a "temple" (see Section 3.6) (Figure 11). Middle Kingdom rock inscriptions also reference religious practices, such as a number of Theban graffiti of Middle Kingdom date that relate to the early history of the Theban festival cycle (Peden, 2001: 29–32).

As with some tombs and temples, several desert sites became places of literary activity, with rock inscriptions recording both pieces known and those otherwise unattested (Darnell, 2013a: 81). Desert, travel, and literature were associated in the minds of at least some educated Egyptians by the time of the Middle Kingdom (Darnell, et al., 2002: 147 and pl. 112; Parkinson, 2002: 61 and 73). Rock inscription and rock art sites could be places of spontaneous literary composition, probably oral, epigraphic, and musical (Morel, 2021).[20] A site in the desert hinterland of Qamula represents an elaborate collection of texts and depictions deriving from a tradition of creativity in the liminal desert region (see Section 3.6).

Rock inscriptions can include curses against those that would erase or damage the inscription (Žaba, 1974: nos. 24, 56, 57, 58), evidence for the importance and memorializing aspects of some rock inscriptions. The permanent nature of rock inscriptions at times inspired funerary references, such as the *ḥtp di nswt*, "an offering that the king gives," formulae (Hintze & Reineke, 1989: 37, passim; Darnell, et al., 2002: 95). Rock inscriptions could serve apotropaic functions, even recording spells for magical protection, and simply viewing or reading texts may offer a promise of health and safety (see Section 3.9). A demotic inscription in the Wadi Hammamat records a magical spell for protection against scorpions, apparently for the benefit of travelers who might not have the appropriate text in copy or memory (Vittmann, 2003: 118–119).

3.6 Shrines Natural and Constructed

Some travelers may have ventured into the desert alone in order to have a personal religious experience in a liminal area. In Theban Graffito No.

---

[20] Darnell, et al., 2002: 107–119 and pls. 85–88 (WHRI 8), inspired by Sinuhe's praise of Senwosret I. For a depiction of a singing man playing an asymmetrical lyre, perhaps a record of a desert performance, see Darnell, et al., 2002: 93–94 (WHRI 3).

Figure 11 The rock inscription site of Vulture Rock within the Wadi Hilal; inset:
an Old Kingdom priest's inscription, with rectangle highlighting the phrase
"this temple"

1394, in the Wadi Sikket Taga Zeid far to the west on the southern shoulder of
the Qurn, the peak above the Valley of the Kings, a visitor to the site in the Late
Ramesside Period wrote: "Come to me, oh Amun, come and save, while I am in
the mountains."[21] In Theban Graffito No. 904, the supplicant imperatively calls
to Amun: "Turn your heart toward me" (Spiegelberg, 1921: no. 904; Darnell,
2013a: 63). Desert sites with formal temple architecture, like the temple of Seti
I in the Wadi Mia at el-Kanais, could also attract later inscriptions recording
prayers for salvation and thanks for a safe return (Adams, 2011: 153–164).

A far more elaborate place of personal worship and appeal to both deities and
potential later visitors is the rock inscription site in the desert west of modern
Qamula (Figure 12) where a priest named Pahu transformed a rock shelf into his
personal shrine (Darnell, 2013a: 7–82 and pls. 1–73), paleographically and
iconographically datable to about the reign of Amenhotep II (1427–1400
BCE). Pahu's imagery blends temple-like scenes appropriate to standard temple
iconography with unusual inscriptions of personal recollections and direct
address to those who might visit the site. Pahu records a prayer he spoke to

---

[21] Černý, 1956: pl. 75, no. 1394; also pl. 64, no. 1345; for parallels in other hymns, including Pahu's
prayer to Amun, see Darnell, 2013a: 31–32.

Figure 12 Inscription site of the priest Pahu (west of Qamula); bottom left: annotated images of the king Ahmose and goddess Taweret (horizontal text states that he made it "for himself"); bottom right: Pahu libating and censing before the goddess Hathor

Amun during a storm at sea, and depicts himself offering to the goddess Hathor while admonishing any reading his inscriptions to have pure thoughts when they make offerings in the temple.

Although a number of other New Kingdom rock inscriptions record hymns and prayers (most addressed to Amun, e.g., Spiegelberg, 1921: nos. 904 and 914; Černy, 1956: nos. 1345 and 1394), and injunctions to personal piety (Černy, 1956: no. 1396), Pahu's inscriptions appear to be among the earliest clear indications of the personal piety that will become such a feature of

Ramesside Period Egyptian religion (Luiselli, 2011). Rock inscriptions in a desert environment enabled personal expressions of piety, providing an opportunity for a more formal but idiosyncratic expression of personal religion that no other space in ancient Egypt provided until considerably later in the New Kingdom. Pahu refers to a number of his productions as having been made by him for himself. Nevertheless, he also directly addresses visitors in at least one inscription. Even within what appears to have been a personal shrine, Pahu conformed to some extent to the more usual public orientation of ancient Egyptian rock art and rock inscriptions.

Pahu did not attempt to transform his site, either through the construction of any dry-stone walls, or the carving of an architectural element at the shelf. Like the Gebel Agg shrine near Toshka (Van Siclen, 1997: 409–416), the natural architecture of Pahu's shrine is a ledge with rocky overhang on a natural desert eminence. Other features, like the so-called Hathor Rock at Faras, might both attract inscriptions and apparently become a local cult focus (Pinch, 1993: 28–40). Rock inscriptions of cultic significance may also cluster at an area providing shade and something of a natural "shrine," as at the *Paneia* of the Coptos to Berenike route (Colin, 1998).

As well as adapting a cave or rock overhang, the creators of natural desert shrines could also focus on small dry-stone constructions (Williams, 2006; Darnell & Manassa, 2013). A stone enclosure with associated monuments may serve as a sanctuary in its own right, augmenting a natural shelf or other feature. Such a rectilinear dry-stone structure, incorporating as its back wall a rock overhang, served as a Hathoric temple for the New Kingdom quarry at Timna in the Arabeh; the site incorporates some more formal architectural elements, smaller monuments and votive objects, and is associated with a large rock inscription (Rothenberg, 1988; 1993). At Gebel Tingar on the west bank of Aswan, a walled courtyard encompassing a large boulder formed a setting for both free-standing monuments and rock inscriptions (Jaritz, 1981: 241–246). A similar wall encloses the rock shrine of Gebel Agg, near Toshka, the ceramic remains and inscriptions of which suggest that it might have been a particularly important religious site for Medjoy Nubians (Trigger, 1996: 804, 806, fig. 3).

Old Kingdom rock inscriptions in the Wadi Hilal attest to visits by priests to a desert temple (see Section 3.5). The priestly inscriptions focus on a massive free-standing segment of the higher rocky desert, known today as "Vulture Rock," that rises abruptly from the floor of the Wadi Hilal. At the southeast corner of Vulture Rock and a lower rocky outcropping to the southeast, the inscriptions are densest. A small number of inscriptions at both sites mention "this temple," although no surviving evidence of any built Old Kingdom temple survives in the wadi. Considerable ceramic material of Old Kingdom date, consistent with the remains of festival activities, is present on the eastern end of the lower outcropping, and similar ceramic material and remains of small monuments such as offering tables – all of Old Kingdom date – are known from the wadi below the later Eighteenth Dynasty temple farther to the southeast.

Stairs cut into the top of Vulture Rock, and steps excavated down into a natural wadi bed just to the north of the outcropping, mimic Egyptian temple architecture: steps to the roof of a temple for astronomical observations on one hand, and steps into a sacred lake for ritual ablutions on the other. No evidence has thus far been recovered that enables the stairs atop Vulture Rock to be dated to the Old Kingdom, although such an early date is possible. The existence of the sets of stairs indicates a temple-like use of the Wadi Hilal, suggesting an interpretation of the Old Kingdom priests' references to "this temple" as designating the desert landscape, Vulture Rock itself, as a temple.

A Predynastic depiction of the traditional Upper Egyptian shrine (the *Per-Wer*) on Vulture Rock may be evidence for semi-permanent structures in the Wadi Hilal at an early date, and the ceramic material and small stone objects of later, Old Kingdom date may have once occupied small tent-like or mud brick structures located at various points in the wadi. The specification of the rock as "this temple," however, suggests that the Wadi Hilal was a sacred landscape that could be augmented by architecture, but for which the oldest and most impressive foci were natural elements of the landscape. The Wadi Hilal continued to be a ritually charged landscape, and by the Eighteenth Dynasty a small temple structure appears, augmented by a speos of Ramesside date, with small satellite temple, the small rock-cut temple ultimately becoming a more elaborate hemispeos during the Ptolemaic Period (Derchain, 1971).

3.7 The Hemispeos

At a number of desert sites, including the temple of Seti I at el-Kanais in the Wadi Abbad/Wadi Mia in the Eastern Desert (Figure 13), the temple of Smithis in the Wadi Hilal, and numerous locations in the Kharga and Dakhla Oases, as far away as the temple of Amun in Siwa Oasis, ancient Egyptian rulers constructed formal temples. The deities associated with these endowments are often those connected with the road(s) with which the temple was associated (Figure 14). So the deities of temples in Kharga and Dakhla are often associated with a Nile Valley religious center, frequently a temple at the Nilotic terminus of the desert road with which the oasis temple is itself associated (Darnell, Klotz,

Figure 13 Hemispeos temple of Seti I in Wadi Kanais

& Manassa, 2013). Whereas the major temples of the oases were free-standing structures, temples on desert roads, such as the temples of Kanais and Smithis, were partially rock-cut and partially free-standing structures – hemispeoi, formal versions of the caves and rock overhangs that more private devotional activities in the desert could transform into places of worship.

The Timna shrine (see Section 3.6) represents an intermediary between rock shelters and more elaborate religious architecture. Natural features like rock shelters appear to have been particularly appropriate for worship of the goddess Hathor. A rock cleft at the head of the Valley of the Queens was apparently interpreted as a natural representation of the vulva of the goddess Hathor, receiving only minimal human augmentation, but attracting a number of rock inscriptions.[22] Timna is a smaller and more simplified version of another temple at a quarry site: the Middle Kingdom Serabit el-Khadim temple – dry-stone architecture forming the forward architectural elements fronting a rock-cut shrine (Valbelle & Bonnet, 1996).

Well attested in the temples of Montuhotep II, Hatshepsut, and Thutmose III at Deir el-Bahari, and in the Ramesside through Ptolemaic temple of Smithis in the Wadi Hilal to the east of Elkab, hemispeoi are in essence architectural representations of the returning goddess of the eye of the sun. The hybrid temple – part cut into the mountain, part free-standing – is the architectural

---

[22] Leblanc, 1989: 12; Desroches-Noblecourt, 1995: 24 and pl. 1. For cross-cultural evidence of rock shelters as natural yonic symbols in the landscape see Claassen, 2011: 628–641; Hays-Gilpin, 2004: 65–84.

Figure 14 Plan, view from exterior, and view from interior of the sanctuary of Ghueita Temple in Kharga Oasis; copy of painted decoration from the reign of Darius I on the north wall of the sanctuary, in which the Persian king (facing left) worships Amun, Mut, and Khonsu of Thebes and Min and Isis of Akhmim, emblematic of the Nilotic termini of desert roads from Kharga Oasis to the Nile Valley

version of depictions of the cow of Hathor as Mistress of the West, her hindquarters yet within the slope of the mountain, her forepart emerging into the riverine world of the alluvial land. In the Wadi Hilal, the temple of Smithis emerges from the desert hills, perpendicular to the track leading into the wadi from Elkab; at the juncture of the path from the hemispeos and the roughly east-west route through the Wadi Hilal stands the small temple of Thoth – the deity prepared to welcome and hopefully pacify the goddess as she returns out of the desert into the Nilotic world (Darnell, 1995: 92; 2010: 100–101; 2013: 76–78). Such interactions of humans, monuments, deities, and landscapes are well attested for the topography of the two banks of ancient Thebes (Rummel, 2020).

The hemispeos is also an architectural embodiment of the theology of the returning solar eye goddess – the partially rock-cut temple is the body of the returning goddess,[23] half in the gebel, in the ḫꜣs.t, away and angry in the Red Land, and half emerging into the near desert, on her way to pacification and the Black Land. A number of the speoi and hemispeoi of Upper Egypt and Nubia are also located at the Nile termini of desert tracks (Jacquet, 1967: 91), and proximity to a desert track was probably another consideration for the location of rock overhangs transformed into shrines, such as at Gebel Agg in Nubia and the Pahu shrine near Qamula.

3.8 Cairn Shrines and Cairn Fields

Religious architecture at mines and quarries reveals a continuum of "formality" in which the Egyptians could express their devotion to the king and the deities who would grant a successful mission (names of such appear in Sadek, 1980: 84, ll. 12–13; Espinel, 2005: 65–66). The construction of a constellation of cairns atop a natural ridge defined the sacred space and separated it from the otherwise monotonous physical landscape. The dedication of stelae within these cairns transformed an otherwise blank desert into a religiously charged and inscribed landscape.

Approximately 80 kilometers west-northwest of Toshka in Nubia are the anorthosite gneiss and chalcedony quarries of Gebel el-Asr, commonly known as the Chephren Diorite Quarries (Shaw, et al., 2010). Middle Kingdom expeditions chose a low ridge in the northern environs of the site – Stela Ridge – as a focus for a series of commemorative and votive monuments (Pethen, 2017). These memorials took the form of dry-stone cairns, small arms of which created rudimentary courtyards, in at least some of which the expeditions set up stelae and other small stone monuments (Figure 15). In the relatively flat landscape of the region, the small cairn-shrines atop a low ridge substituted for the rock-cut shrines present at other quarries. During the late Middle Kingdom and the Second Intermediate Period, miners at Gebel Zeit, on the Red Sea coast, constructed similar dry-stone enclosures as foci for votive objects (Pinch, 1993: 73–74; Régen & Soukiassian, 2008: 1–7). In a non-quarry setting, cairn

---

[23] For the temple as body of the deity, see *i.a.* Finnestad, 1997.

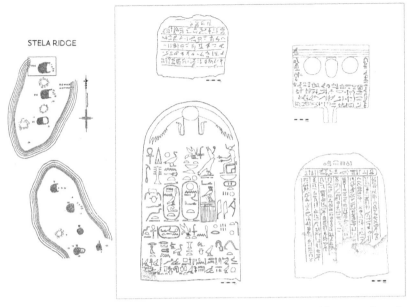

Figure 15 Plan of the "Stela Ridge" cairn shrines at the Nubian quarries of Gebel el-Asr, with drawings of the four monuments from Cairn VIII (plan after Engelbach, 1939)

shrines appear atop Gebel Antef, on the Theban West Bank, in conjunction with a now destroyed sandstone chapel of Seventeenth Dynasty date.

Cairn VIII at Gebel el-Asr (Engelbach, 1939: pl. LIV) may serve as an example of the material associated with the cairn shrines (Darnell & Manassa, 2013). The four objects at Cairn VIII relate to expeditions during regnal years 4 and 6 of Amenemhat III and differ considerably in size and formality: a round-top stela of regnal year 4, inscribed with a text in hieroglyphic script with some hieratic features; a small rectangular stela with a lapidary hieratic script, dated regnal year 4; a round-top stela of regnal year 6, with a depiction of the goddess Hathor and the Horus name of the king within the lunette; and a sandstone offering table. The objects reveal a revisiting of the monuments of an earlier expedition by later visitors. The offering table, inviting future visitors to pour a libation for the benefit of those mentioned in the inscriptions, and an "address to the living" formula on the regnal year 6 stela, demonstrate an expectation of continued engagement with the cairn shrine and its ensemble of monuments.

Cairn shrines with associated, free-standing monuments, like the ensembles at Gebel el-Asr, can also appear in the environs of a more formal temple structure, as at Serabit el-Khadim. Some of the large stelae along the approach to the temple of Hathor at Serabit el-Khadim were set up within low, circular, dry-stone enclosures (Valbelle & Bonnet, 1996: 70–71), similar to those at Gebel el-Asr. The enclosures with stelae at Serabit, like the Gebel el-Asr cairn shrines, presuppose the presence of worshippers. The stela of Sobekherheb, with offering table on the ground in front, at one side of an enclosure of stones (Petrie, 1906: 66, ill. 78–80; Valbelle & Bonnet, 1996: 29 *et passim*), invites visitors to occupy the otherwise empty space within the enclosure – the ensemble is incomplete without a human visitor. Desert memorials at Serabit el-Khadim, Gebel el-Asr, and elsewhere insert the visitor into the position and role of dedicator, officiant, and maintainer of the deeds of the one(s) who made the shrine and those who are memorialized on the monuments therein. These desert assemblages are not passive memorials, but actuators of future human activity.

The varying positions of the men who dedicated the monuments at Gebel el-Asr, and the varying sizes and stylistic features of those monuments, parallel similar assemblages of stelae from the more formal and Nilotic settings of the Terrace of the Great God at Abydos (O'Connor, 2009: 92–96; Yamamoto, 2015) and the Heqaib sanctuary at Elephantine (Franke, 1994). Ranging from palm-sized stelae with a few names in hieratic, to large and carefully executed hieroglyphic stelae, the Abydos monuments commemorate both family members and the more extended "work families" of professional colleagues, the latter paralleling the Gebel el-Asr material.[24]

Ensembles of texts, especially in the combination of "autobiographical" stelae and offering tables, also appear at all three sites (Gebel el-Asr, Abydos, and Serabit el-Khadim).[25] Each monument both fills a function for the dedicant, and at the same time provides a place for coworkers and subordinates to offer their own votive objects. The stelae and other inscribed monuments transformed the cairns at Gebel el-Asr from temporary religious structures for the use of their builders into more permanent religious installations, perpetually actuated by the presence of the living worshippers who will interact with them in future visits to the sites. The monuments in the cairn shrines at Gebel el-Asr created a religious and physical landscape that ensured the continued commemoration of the miners at the site, and their spiritual participation at future cultic activities.

Between Stela Ridge, the site of the cairn shrines at Gebel el-Asr, and the track to Toshka (Shaw, 2006: 253–266), is Twenty-Cairn Ridge, crowned with numerous small dry-stone cairns, without associated inscribed material. Similar

---

[24] Leprohon, 1978: 33–38; note the ability of work subordinates to fulfill the role of *sem*-priest on Thirteenth Dynasty Abydene stelae – see Franke, 2003: 73–75.

[25] Hölzl, 2002: 141–142 (to the list add the example from Sinai in Valbelle & Bonnet, 1996: 155, fig. 180).

clusters of small cairns appear at several sites in the Eastern and Western Deserts (Darnell & Manassa, 2013: 56–57, 90; Darnell, in press c). Unlike the intervisible line-of-sight cairns marking a number of desert roads, particularly in areas otherwise lacking natural landmarks, these clusters of small stone piles appear at the termini of roads, and at points having particular religious significance.

Such cairn fields appear to be evidence of votive activities at the termini of desert roads, perhaps dedicated by travelers thanking the gods for their safe return. At Gebel el-Asr, the ridge of cairns is devoid of inscribed material, suggesting that the cairn fields may be anepigraphic markers, corresponding to the rock art and rock inscriptions of some sites, and the cairn shrines and inscribed monuments of others. Votive cairns may represent physical *vestigia* of both travelers at sites without surfaces suitable for inscribing, and those visitors without the ability to leave a textual or clear representational mark. What might be dismissed as a collection of vertically oriented stones is another demonstration of the spiritual significance of the desert landscape.

3.9 The Ruler as Intercessor in the Desert

Although many may seem informal, the results of anything but official sponsorship and influence, a number of desert graffiti played roles in supporting the official social and religious order. Already during the Naqada II Period (ca. 4000–3500 BCE), rock inscriptions record tableaux of royal ritual power, and reveal the interactions of royalty and divinity (Darnell, 2009). The formal rock inscription tableau of Montuhotep II in the Wadi Schatt er-Rigal (Figure 16) may provide evidence for the existence already during the Eleventh Dynasty of the "Theban version" of the doctrine of the divine birth of the king, well before the earliest explicit text referring to the same (Darnell, 2004a: 26–28). Rock inscriptions also represent some of the most distant memorials of pharaonic Egyptian power, including an inscription of Montuhotep II in the environs of Gebel Uweinat at the southeastern corner of modern Egypt (Förster, 2015: 479–487) and an inscription of Ramesses III near the oasis of Tayma, in the northeastern portion of modern Saudi Arabia (Sperveslage, 2016: 305–306).

A rock inscription could indicate that the viewing of an image or reading of an inscription would benefit other travelers. A Middle Kingdom inscription in the Wadi el-Hol (possibly made by the priest who carved a lengthier and adjacent inscription) depicted the statue of a ruler (standing atop a transport sledge) above a horizontal line of text: "As for the one who will read these

Figure 16 Shatt er-Rigal inscription of Montuhotep II

writings, he will reach (home) in peace" (Darnell, et al., 2002: 103). A king could also set up an actual statue on a desert road, inscribed with magico-religious spells, the reading of which will help travelers, and such a traveler might carve a similar spell (against scorpions), in order to provide the same benefit. Ramesses III set up a healing statue to the east of Gebel Ahmar (Drioton, 1939), now subsumed in the sprawl of modern Cairo, at a point where a traveler on the desert road would catch a first or last glimpse of the Nile Valley proper. A later traveler on the Wadi Hammamat road in the Eastern Desert carved a text against scorpions, apparently with a similar purpose (Vittmann, 2003: 118–119).

The Middle Kingdom depiction in the Wadi el-Hol and the statue of Ramesses III from Gebel Ahmar share the concept of the beneficence of royal statuary, and representations of the divine ruler, at desert sites. By the time of the Middle Kingdom, both two- and three-dimensional depictions of the ruler were important elements of devotion at desert sites. At Shatt er-Rigal, a towering sunk relief image of Montuhotep II, visually evoking the concept of the divine birth of the king, has the scale and technical sophistication of a temple relief, and a commensurate ritual function. In the Gebel el-Asr cairn shrines, small stone images of falcons bear the Horus names of Senwosret II and Amenemhat III (Darnell & Manassa, 2013: 57), and similar statues were deposited at the quarry sites of Serabit el-Khadim and Gebel Zeit (Pethen, 2014). The chief deities in the material from Gebel el-Asr, Gebel Zeit, and Serabit el-Khadim are the goddess Hathor and the god Horus, with the ruler, most prominently as a manifestation of the latter.[26]

4 Writing and Drawing in the Desert

The late Paleolithic art of the Kom Ombo-Aswan region (the Qurta images have a minimum age of approximately 15,000 calendar years – Huyge, 2013; Huyge & Claes, 2012) and the considerably later Epipaleolithic depictions of probable fish weirs at el-Hosh (perhaps as early as 5600 BCE – Huyge, 1998) are remarkable earlier examples of inscribing the desert landscapes bordering the Nile Valley, but they do not appear to influence the art of the later Predynastic Period and Dynasty 0. The rock art traditions of Gebel Uweinat and the Gilf Kebir (Förster, Riemer & Kuper, 2013; Kuper, et al., 2013) in the far southwest, the abstract iconography of Abka, Bir Nakheila, and Rayayna (Darnell, D., 2002: 160–161), and the painted handprints of Farafra (Huyge, 2003: 67–68) and Rayayna (Darnell, D., 2002: 161, pls. 90–91; Darnell 2009: 86–87) appear equally unrelated to the later and continuous iconographic traditions of Upper Egypt and Lower Nubia.

Many concentrations of early rock art occur in the Eastern Desert, associated with routes between the Nile Valley and the Red Sea,[27] and in the Western Desert, located near the Nile Valley and the western oases, and along the routes interconnecting those areas.[28] As important as the Predynastic rock art of the Egyptian deserts is in its own right, it holds a special significance for the light it sheds on the origins of writing. The numinous deserts of Egypt and Nubia, attracting rock art and later rock inscriptions, became crucibles for the development of writing systems in northeast Africa.

The earliest writing in Africa, perhaps the earliest fully developed writing system incorporating phonetic indicators of a specific language, appears in its developmental stage in Upper Egypt about 3250 BCE, at the cusp of the Predynastic and Protodynastic Periods. That time, the beginning of Dynasty 0, is a period of increasing administrative complexity and cultural unity in Upper Egypt (Campagno, 2013). The first attestations of the nascent Egyptian writing system appear on small objects from an early ruler's burial (Tomb U-j) at Abydos, and in a large-scale early hieroglyphic inscription on the surface of a rock face at el-Khawy (7 km north of Elkab) (Figure 17). The origins of this script begin already during the Naqada II Period, as an essentially cosmographic imagery, in a development best in evidence in the decorated ceramics of Upper

---

[26] Darnell and Manassa, 2013. For Hathor at Gebel Zeit, see the remarks of Régen and Soukiassian, 2008: 51–54; Pinch, 1993: 73.

[27] See Winkler, 1938, 1939; Rothe, Miller, and Rapp, 2008; Judd 2009; Morrow, et al., 2010; Lankester, 2013.

[28] See Darnell, et al., 2002; Darnell, 2013a; Förster, 2015; Lazaridis, 2019; Polkowski, 2018, 2019.

Figure 17 Rock inscription site of El Khawy; inset: early hieroglyphic inscription, ca. 3250 BCE

Egypt, and in the rock art of the Eastern and Western Deserts of Upper Egypt and Lower Nubia.[29]

4.1 Upper Egyptian and Lower Nubian Rock Art of the Fourth Millennium

Beginning around 4000 BCE, rock art proliferates in the deserts of Upper Egypt and Nubia, the iconography concentrating on a limited range of images and themes. The zoomorphic and other images appearing in the art reveal that the ancient artists drew not so much what they were seeing, but more often what they were thinking. During the Naqada II Period (ca. 3500–3250 BCE), both rock art tableaux at desert sites, and the iconography of painted ceramics (Petrie's Decorated Ware) and small decorated objects, frequently juxtapose desert and Nilotic imagery. Balancing the desert and riverine worlds of the Egyptian cosmos through iconography, Predynastic artists at desert sites could Niloticize and socialize the desert hinterlands of the Nile Valley (Darnell, 2007; Riemer & Förster, 2013), reconciling the two biomes of the Egyptian and Nubian worlds in potent symbiosis (Darnell, 2009: 87–88). Already during the Predynastic Period, earlier rock art images attracted similar works by later visitors, in a form of iconographic attraction.

---

[29] This section is a summary of Darnell, 2020b.

One focus of the predominantly zoomorphic imagery of early Egyptian rock art is on animals representing aspects of the cosmic cycle (Huyge, 2002). Essentially supplanting earlier zoomorphic images in importance, depictions of watercraft become increasingly common over the course of the Naqada II Period. The image of a boat may appear as an addition to an earlier zoomorphic representation, and a combination of boat with animal depiction, all of a single carving event, also occurs (Darnell, 2009: 90–91). Standards and deck structures, more consistent with ritual barks than with mundane water craft, frequently appear in rock art depictions of vessels.

Hunting, especially of animals either dangerous or difficult to hunt (e.g., barbary sheep and hippopotami), and those rare at best in the actual landscapes of Upper Egypt (e.g., giraffes and elephants) are often more ubiquitous in the iconography than representations of the gazelle and other small game that would have been more abundant in the Upper Egyptian and Lower Nubian desert landscapes (Hendrickx, et al., 2010). Rock art thus focuses on animals with cosmic meaning (e.g., the giraffe may possess a solar significance) or prestige game animals who would then become ritual offerings at Nilotic sites (Graff, Eyckerman, & Hendrickx, 2011). Although not always directly depicted, hunters are frequently present in the form of ropes attached to captured animals, in the presence of other objects of human manufacture, or in the appearance of canids whose hunting activities can represent human society (Darnell, 2011: 1171–1173; 2014: 122–123).

The motifs of the elite hunt and ritual meat offering also appear as decoration on the bodies of the hunters, and the female ritualists who oversaw the translation of the animals of the hunt into the victuals of the gods at early temple sites. These graffiti-related images appear as tattoos and perhaps body painting that linked the human actors in both the desert and the Nile Valley to the cycle of events in which they participated, a ritual hunt that connected desert and Nile (Darnell, 2018; see reference section 3.2). As the desert skin could reflect the events that occurred in the two biomes of elite activity, so the skins of some of those elite actors could reflect the desert and Nilotic foci of their ritual cycle.

4.2 The Proto-history of Hieroglyphs: The Development of Iconographic Syntax

Depictions of watercraft, animals, ostriches and ostrich feather fans, female ritualists and their male associates, and a plant-like image that substituted for the female ritualist dominate the iconography of Naqada II Period Decorated Ware vessels (Graff, 2009: 122–124). In the iconography on the Decorated

Ware vessels, predictable associations of images occur. The often large female figure, arms curving up and over the head or lowered to the sides, elbows out, frequently occurs in association with an apparent addax; a vegetal figure representing a female human (Hendrickx & Eyckerman, 2012: 44–46) occurs in conjunction with an animal skin, forming an opposite, inanimate pair to the woman-addax group (Graff, 2009: 91–99).

Other syntactic arrangements appear in late Predynastic iconography. A saddle-billed stork with a serpent rearing beneath its beak represents a composite sign, apparently an icon of "victory," that may appear as the first of a pair of signs, the second apparently qualifying the nature of the victory (Darnell, 2013a: 102, 121). On a late Naqada III (ca. 3200–3100 BCE) decorated comb (Metropolitan Museum of Art, MMA 30.8.224), a giraffe follows the stork and serpent icon, probably an early statement of "solar victory." At the rock inscription site of Gebel Tjauti, a tableau depicts a ruler (perhaps Horus Scorpion of Abydos tomb U-j) brandishing a mace above a bound prisoner; the stork and serpent icon to the right of the group labels the image as a representation of "human victory." Such syntactic arrangements represent the prehistory of writing (Stauder, 2010), a phase rarely in evidence elsewhere, but remarkably well attested in the rock art and proto-inscriptions of the Eastern and Western Deserts of Egypt.

Upper Egyptian and Nubian rock art sites preserve tableaux of a cycle of scenes that may be precursors of the later royal jubilee, a series of rituals ideally celebrated after thirty years of a pharaoh's rule (Darnell, 2009; 2011). Originally identified on decorated objects, textiles, and in the decoration of the important late Naqada II Period Tomb 100 at Hierakonpolis, the images depict a cycle of scenes of hunting, combat, and ritual navigation, ultimately associated with Egyptian kingship (Williams & Logan, 1987; Hendrickx, 2014/15), and representing in essence a ritual realization of the imagery of the early rock art motifs.

In some of these rock art tableaux of royal ritual power, artists employed zoomorphic imagery, nautical iconography, and standard icons from earlier zoomorphic imagery to annotate and explain the depictions those annotations accompany. In one such tableau in the Western Desert (Wadi of the Horus Qa-a, a branch of the Wadi Alamat – Darnell, 2011), bulls as symbols of royal power (Hendrickx, 2002) and canids controlling other animals as images of properly ordered human society triumphing over chaos (Hendrickx, 2006) intermingle with the motifs and iconographic syntax of Decorated Ware vessels. In the Wadi of the Horus Qa-a tableau, a carving of an addax – symbol of meat offerings on Decorated Ware vessels, often paired with the image of a female ritualist – follows and labels the representation of an arrow-pierced human. The resulting image is a syntactically formal statement of the equation of hunting and warfare in Egyptian iconography, already iconographically linked in imagery of the Naqada I Period (Hendrickx, et al., 2010).

The rock art iconographies of Niloticization of the desert and elite hunting practices have combined with the iconographic syntax of Decorated Ware imagery and the icons of nascent royal power to produce annotated depictions of rituals that realize the earlier iconography within human ritual practices. The iconographic corpus of rock art may interact with the iconography and syntax of Decorated Ware ceramics, allowing a syntactic dialog on the surface of the Egyptian deserts.

4.3 Rock Inscriptions and the Earliest Writing in Egypt

Shortly after the development of iconographic syntax, and the use of such imagery to label elements of a larger tableau – as in the Wadi of the Horus Qa-a – the earliest proto-hieroglyphic writing appears in Upper Egypt on small labels from tomb U-j at Abydos, and in the el-Khawy early hieroglyphic rock inscription. Occurring in the burial goods of an early Dynasty 0 royal tomb, the U-j labels demonstrate a use of the nascent script for bureaucratic purposes, and suggest already a ceremonial, ritual, or magico-religious function for early writing in Egypt (Stauder, 2010; Wengrow, 2011), with the colored paste filling the incisions of the signs on the tomb U-j labels giving those objects a prestigious materiality (Stauder, f.c.). The el-Khawy rock inscription demonstrates the importance of the script as demonstrative of power, exerted in the control of prestige goods.

At el-Khawy, on the east bank of the Nile seven kilometers north of Elkab, a large scale rock inscription in early hieroglyphic script (Figure 18) reveals a paleography identical to that of the Abydene labels (Darnell, 2017), indicating a date ca. 3250 BCE. The shared paleography of the el-Khawy inscription and the signs from tomb U-j demonstrates that the inscriptions from both sites represent the beginning of a standardized paleography of the signs that we know from the developed hieroglyphic script. The el-Khawy inscription provides evidence for a public, non-bureaucratic application for the developing script. Incorporating signs from both the ivory label and ceramic annotation corpora in Tomb U-j, the el-Khawy inscription reveals a geographically widespread use of the nascent script, and suggests important connections between Abydos and Elkab/Hierakonpolis at the dawn of Dynasty 0. At el-Khawy, the size (the tallest signs are just over 50 cm) and visibility of an early hieroglyphic inscription support an apotropaic force for the early script, the mere presence of hieroglyphic signs imparting an aura of authority and control, a glamour of prestige.

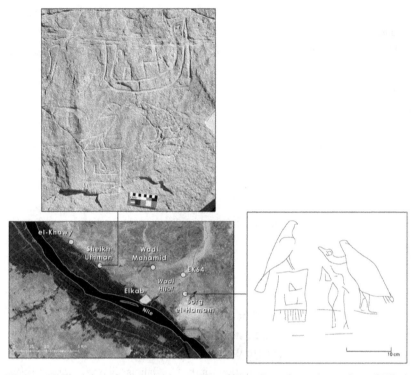

Figure 18 Rock inscriptions with *serekhs* of king Qa-a from the region of Elkab

The el-Khawy inscription especially reveals the final stage in a development from zoomorphic icons of ritual significance to hieroglyphs writing the words and sounds of the ancient Egyptian language. The bucranium on a pole at the right end of the inscription may represent a symbol of royal power, although as a sign it passes out of general hieroglyphic use by the dawn of the Dynastic Period. In the left portion of the inscription, a bald ibis (probable identification) appears between and slightly above two addorsed storks. Later hieroglyphic texts give us the value *ꜣḫ* "to be luminous" and *bꜣ* "power, soul," respectively, for the ibis and stork. The bald ibis in the el-Khawy inscription may then write the root *ꜣḫ*, "to be luminous," thereby both representing the central solar element in the iconography, and at the same time providing a phonetic writing of luminosity. Such a B-A-B arrangement is common to ancient Egyptian depictions of the solar cycle, and the sign of the solar disk between two hills is the Egyptian sign for the horizon, *ꜣḫ.t*, which the el-Khawy group can therefore both depict and write. In the el-Khawy inscription, signs may represent phonemes (bald ibis), terms without phonetic indicators (bucranium on pole), and concepts (addorsed storks as cosmic boundaries), all characteristics of Egyptian hieroglyphic writing.

On a desert cliff at el-Khawy, at the northern edge of a wadi system that accesses the gold mines of the southeastern Egyptian desert, an early king carved a monumental inscription that equated his royal authority with the solar cycle. For the next three millennia, the pharaoh as guarantor of cosmic order would remain central to the theology of Egyptian kingship.

4.4 Setting a Royal Seal on the Desert

With Dynasty 0, the Horus name of the ruler – written in a stylized palace façade, the *serekh*, – begins to appear at desert road sites as a prominent marker of royal interest (Darnell, 2011: 1181). Such *serekh* inscriptions continue through the First Dynasty (Winkler 1938, pl. 11; Žaba, 1974: 239–241; Váhala and Červicek, 1999: no. 149) and into the Second Dynasty (Žaba, 1974: 30–31; Hamilton, 2016), apparently as a means of incorporating within the pharaonic realm a route and the regions and products it accessed. Well attested at and near the termini of several desert roads is the Horus name of Qa-a (ca. 2900 BCE), last king of the First Dynasty (Darnell, 2011: 1181; Darnell & Vanhulle, f.c.). Two of these *serekhs* appear in the region of Elkab (Figure 18), marking the northernmost and southernmost points of direct access to roads that join to the east and lead to the gold mining regions of the Eastern Desert. A probable *serekh* of Qa-a in the northern portion of Kharga Oasis demonstrates the king's interest in desert roads far beyond the Nile Valley (Ikram & Rossi, 2004).

The Egyptians conceptualized these royal inscriptions as "sealing" the desert. The Qa-a *serekhs* near Elkab are associated with an image of the vulture goddess Nekhbet; and the southern inscription, at the Borg el-Hammam, also incorporates a short hieroglyphic text that is arranged identically to contemporaneous seal impressions (Darnell & Vanhulle, f.c.). The iconography associated with sealing is reinforced by the use of the verb *ḥtm* "to seal" to describe a ruler's annexation of a road in an inscription of late First Intermediate Period date (ca. 2100 BCE) (Darnell, et al., 2002: 30–34). The relative proliferation of Early Dynastic *serekhs* implies the presence of treasury officials, early representatives of the "sealers of the god" (*ḥtmty-nṯr*) (Kuraszkiewicz, 2006).

At Nag el-Hamdulab, northwest of Elephantine, the figure of a ruler wearing the White Crown (the traditional crown of Upper Egypt) supervises a nautical procession with images of domination of foreigners. A hieroglyphic inscription of apparently early First Dynasty date (ca. 3100 BCE) labels the scene as a representation of the Following of Horus (the royal entourage) and a record of the taxation of an area at the terminus of a desert road (Darnell, Hendrickx, & Gatto, 2017). The newly established royal authority literally steps into the earlier image of Nilotic festival activities that proliferated at desert sites during the Upper Egyptian Predynastic Period.

5 Self-Presentation of Foreigners in the Egyptian Deserts

In previous sections, the primary focus has been Egypto-centric: Egyptian administration of the desert; Egyptian worship in the desert; Egyptian creation of a hieroglyphic script. This final section presents some of the ways in which foreigners also engaged with the deserts of Sinai, Egypt, and Nubia. Broken ceramics bear mute witness to their presence on road networks. Some of these foreigners were members of Egyptian-led expeditions, while others, like the Nubian families surveilled in the Semna Dispatches (see Section 2.3), were not necessarily part of the Egyptian world. Yet all of these groups also interacted with the desert landscape, and the products of those interactions often illuminate self-presentation of foreigners absent from Nilotic settings.

5.1 Nubians and Egyptians

As early as the Protodynastic and Early Dynastic Periods (Somaglino & Tallet, 2014, 2015), Egyptian expeditions left records within Nubia, while at the same time, Upper Egypt and Lower Nubia shared an early iconography of rulership (Williams & Logan, 1987; Darnell, 2013a: 123; Brémont & Vanhulle, in press). Although a form of religious conversion seems to correspond to the adoption of Egyptian script by elite Nubians of the Pharaonic Period (Doyen & Gabolde, 2017), at least occasional examples of Nubian self-expression – left by people who were not members of the most exalted echelons of society – appear in the rock art and inscriptions of the Egyptian deserts. The Egyptian-Nubian cultural entanglement so clearly in evidence by the time of the New Kingdom (Van Pelt, 2013; Raue, 2019) is present in rock art much earlier.

In a series of autobiographical rock inscriptions at Nag el-Wasiya, south of Aswan in the region of Abisko, a Nubian soldier Tjehemau described his career in the Egyptian military, from his meeting with Montuhotep II through a period of internal conflict, possibly during the reign of Amenemhat I (Darnell, 2004a: 23–37). Tjehemau is an example of the Nubian auxiliaries who assisted the Middle Kingdom state in exerting authority over desert regions (Moreno Garcia, 2010: 27–29). Composed in good Middle Egyptian and of no mean literary merit, Tjehemau's inscription presents its subject as a Nubian who contrasts himself with what he depicts as a timid Theban army, whose commander he nevertheless supports (Inscription No. 1, ll. 9–16):

He (the king) traversed the entire land, having decided to slaughter the 'Amu of Djaty,
When it approached, Thebes was in flight. It was the Nubian who brought about the rally.

Tjehemau also compares himself to the Egyptian ruler (Inscription No. 3, ll. 15–18):

Tjehemau the victorious sailed north like the lion, Son of Re, *bity*-king, together with this army of his which he recruited.

Claiming to be braver than the Egyptians he supports, Tjehemau is an outsider without whom the Theban insider could neither hold nor expand, writing an early version of a "ripping yarn," a form of literature known from more recent imperial systems (Dixon, 1994). Later Tjehemau depicts his arrival at Thebes during a festival as though the city had assembled in his honor (Inscription No. 4, l. 1–Inscription No. 5, l. 2).

A site of New Kingdom date (probably Eighteenth Dynasty) near the Wadi Alamat Road, northwest of ancient Thebes (SWA 1), preserves depictions of Nubian soldiers in a festival context (Figure 19). The Nubian figures are carved alongside a pseudo-inscription and inaccurate copies of short inscriptions probably derived from glyptic (preliminary treatment in Darnell, 2002b: 143–144). The depictions of Nubian soldiers there are grouped near the drawings of what may be the bark of Amun, recalling the actual appearance of Nubian soldiers in conjunction with Theban festivals (as in Epigraphic Survey, 1996: 16, pl. 32). Also present at the site SWA 1 are a few divine images, depictions of horses, and a scene of a family of three lions, the largest standing atop a supine human.

Depictions of ritual activities are present in New Kingdom Nubian rock art as well – at Korosko images of wrestlers (on Nubian wrestlers, Decker, 1991: 97–105) occur in conjunction with the depiction of a seated official observing dancers, and the representation of a lion standing atop a prone human, facing a feather-wearing warrior armed with axe and rectangular shield (Dunbar, 1940: pl. 19; imperfect drawings in Váhala & Cervicek, 1999: pls. 119–120 [nos. 456, 458, 459, and 461]; Suková, 2011: 148–149).

The festival imagery that appealed to Tjehemau, and provided the basis for imagery at SWA 1 and at the Korosko site, links rock art and inscriptions of Nubians with military careers. Service in expeditions of military and quarrying natures could provide Nubians with paths to Egyptianization (Darnell, 2013b: 791–792, with nn. 31–32), but Nubian identity did not necessarily vanish. Tjehemau in particular highlights his hybrid nature. Like the Inca in their imagery and ritual performances in colonial Peru (Dean, 1999), in order to mediate alterity for Nubians and Egyptians alike, the Nubian soldiers who left their inscriptions emphasize their inherently conflicted (compare Dean, 1999: 122–159) composite culture. That same entangled culture is archaeologically in evidence in the persistence of Nubian foodways at late Middle Kingdom settlements in the oases (see Section 2.4).

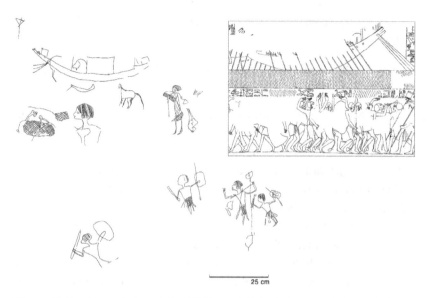

25 cm

Figure 19 Rock inscription site of SWA-1, with depictions of Nubian soldiers in a possible festival procession; inset: Nubian soldiers from the Opet Festival scenes of Luxor Temple (reign of Tutankhamun; after Wreszinski, 1935: pl. 200)

Tjehemau could command the resources for the carving of Middle Egyptian hieratic inscriptions, their signs monumental in comparison with other rock inscriptions. The Nubian soldiers at SWA 1 who created a place in the desert where they could commemorate their own participations in festivals used images and psuedo-texts. Nubian self-presentation in the desert could deploy Egyptian hieroglyphic script or figural art, but in both cases the men retain their Nubian identity. Tjehemau is the "Nubian," braver than his Egyptian compatriots; at site SWA 1, the carved human figures display clear Nubian cultural markers.

Egyptian self-presentation in the desert displays a similar continuum, from hieroglyphic inscriptions, at times even sophisticated literary forms, to a clearly written name and title in the cursive hieratic script, to incised signs resembling pot marks and other pseudo-hieroglyphs. This final group of pseudo-writing may, considering the parallels in pot marks and seals, relate to the control of resources at desert sites, and products traveling along the desert roads.

5.2 Lapidary Hieratic and the Origins of the Alphabet

Not all groups operating within the desert hinterlands of Egypt appear to have adapted Egyptian imagery to their inscriptions. Whereas Nubian culture engaged with Egyptian iconography and ideology from an early date, even adopting Egyptian language and scripts for both private and royal inscriptions, the people of the northeastern hinterland of the Nile Delta did not frequently follow suit. As rock inscriptions at sites in the Western Desert and in the Sinai peninsula reveal, the "Western Asiatic" auxiliaries of the ancient Egyptians borrowed hieratic and hieroglyphic signs, but not the Egyptian language.

Old Kingdom and Middle Kingdom scribes accompanying desert expeditions developed a loosely standardized script for rock inscriptions (Vandekerckhove & Müller-Wollermann, 2001: 347–349; Ali, 2002: 12–22). The script blended cursive hieratic and hieroglyphic features of signs, which decreased the time needed to carve a hieroglyphic monument, while maintaining a graphic formality greater than a purely hieratic inscription. Particularly suited to the medium of a natural stone surface, this 'lapidary hieratic' script was used by scribes traveling with expeditions into the Egyptian and Nubia desert to memorialize their activities (Gratien, 2004).

During the late Twelfth Dynasty, a 'proto-alphabetic' script appears in rock inscriptions and on small objects, principally in Sinai – most prominently at the site of Serabit el-Khadim – and at the Wadi el-Hol in the Theban Western Desert (Darnell & Dobbs-Allsopp, et al., 2005; Hamilton, 2006). The *abgad* script, an alphabet that omits vowels, has been termed "Proto-Sinaitic," and perhaps more descriptively Early Alphabetic. The somewhat roughly made signs in the Sinai *abgad* inscriptions represent versions of hieroglyphic prototypes, whereas the signs in the two Early Alphabetic inscriptions in the Wadi el-Hol derive from lapidary hieratic prototypes. The Early Alphabetic script employed Egyptian signs, each representing a single phoneme through acrophony from the Semitic-language name of the object (Darnell & Dobbs-Allsopp, et al., 2005; Hamilton, 2006).

Desert roads were both caravan routes and lines of communication traveled by messengers on foot, with some mounted on horseback by the New Kingdom (see Section 2.5). A hieratic rock inscription at the Wadi el-Hol, dating to the reign of Amenemhat III (ca. 1831–1786 BCE), lists the names of couriers (*sỉnw*) and royal messengers (*wpwty-nsw.t*), alongside a "General of Asiatics" (*ỉmy-r mšᶜ ᶜȝm.w*) (Darnell & Dobbs-Allsopp, et al., 2005: 85–90, 102–106). Asiatic auxiliary troops and affiliated scribes were also present in the Sinai, the other location of the Early Alphabetic script (Valbelle & Bonnet, 1996: 34–35, 147). The creation of the earliest *abgad* texts appears to result from the interaction of Egyptian scribes and Asiatic expeditionary forces during the Middle Kingdom (*contra* Goldwasser, 2006). This *abgad* is the direct predecessor of Old Canaanite, the first in a line of paleographic development that gives rise to modern alphabets.

6 Conclusion

Egypt's desert hinterlands were not passive and blank spaces through which the ancient Egyptians roamed at will, nor were they forbidding wastes haunted by frightful monsters. Instead, this Element has shown how the ancient Egyptians viewed the desert landscape as a living entity, with which they could engage in a visual dialog (Section 3). The marking of the desert with rock art and later inscriptions, socializing the desert and creating places in otherwise vast and nameless spaces, could find a reflection in the decoration of the human body, the skins of humans and rocks reflecting one another. In developing themes of rock art, visitors to desert sites could engage with other humans, past, contemporaneous, and to come. Within this conjunction of interacting bodies the ancient Egyptians developed and expanded concepts of iconographic syntax that provide a precursor to the hieroglyphic writing system (Section 4).

Within the liminal desert landscape, the ancient Egyptians interacted with deities, who might travel through the dry borderlands of the Nile Valley. Temples could architecturally reflect the returning solar eye goddess, and worshippers could meet and even accompany her back to the Nile Valley. Humans within the desert vastness might feel themselves within a sacred landscape, as this Element has demonstrated. Within the desert, a priest could transcend the decorum expected in the Nile Valley to create a personal shrine. Similarly, desert shrines at sites visited as part of officially sponsored missions may be the focus for stelae, statues, and other small monuments. These formal structures exist alongside votive cairns commemorating non-literate travelers. Self-presentation in the desert for Nubians and Egyptians alike, frequently in the context of ritual events, complements evidence from the Nile Valley.

Control of the deserts by the nascent Egyptian state led to early applications of the hieroglyphic script to mark royal control of desert roads and their resources (Section 2). Throughout the Pharaonic Period, Egyptian desert interactions reveal attempts not simply to control an outer realm, but to transform at least some portions of the outer desert hinterlands into integral elements of the Egyptian state. The development of a dual system of oversight for desert expeditions, some officials operating within a chain of command and others reporting more directly to high levels of the administration, reveals the flexibility of ancient Egyptian bureaucracy.

This Element has presented the ways in which the Egyptians physically controlled the desert landscape, especially the roads that connected the Nile Valley with distant locales and provided access between points along the river. Particular focus has been given to the role of Nubians in desert administration, culminating with Nubian self-presentation within the desert landscape (Section 5).

No study of ancient Egypt is complete without a consideration of the vast expanses of desert east and west of the Nile Valley. This Element will hopefully provide scholars of Egypt and the ancient world more generally with a point of departure for understanding the complex interactions of Egypt and the desert.

Bibliography

Adams, C. (2011). Travel and the Perception of Space in the Eastern Desert of Egypt. In M. Rathmann, ed., *Wahrnehmung und Erfassung geographischer Räume in der Antike*. Mainz am Rhein: Philipp von Zabern, pp. 211–220.

Ali, M. S. (2002). *Hieratische Ritzinschriften aus Theben. Göttinger Orientforschung IV/34*. Wiesbaden: Harrassowitz.

Ashby, S. (2018). Dancing for Hathor: Nubian Women in Egyptian Cultic Life. *Dotawo: A Journal of Nubain Studies* 5: 63–90.

Aston, D. (1996). Sherds from a Fortified Townsite near Abu 'Id. *Cahiers de la céramique égyptienne* 4: 19–39.

Aufrère, S. (1991). *L'univers minéral dans la pensée égyptienne 1 – L'influence du desert et des minéraux sur la mentalité des anciens Égyptiens*, Cairo: Institut Français d'Archéologie Orientale.

Aufrère, S. (1999b). L'Étrange et la curiosité: mineraux, coquillages, fossils, meteorites et plantes curieuses dans les mentalities des anciens Égyptiens et des habitants du desert (autour de l'Univers mineral IX). In S. Aufrère, ed., *Encyclopédie religieuses de l'Univers vegetal 1: croyances phytoreligieuses de l'Égypte ancienne*, Montpellier: Université Paul Valéry-Montpellier III, pp. 69–85.

Aufrère, S. (2007). *Thot Hermès l'Égyptien: de l'infiniment grand à l'infiniment petit*, Paris: L'Harmattan.

Bard, K. A. and Fattovich, R. (2018). *Seafaring Expeditions to Punt in the Middle Kingdom: excavations at Mersa/Wadi Gawasis, Egypt*. Leiden: Brill.

Bardinet, T. (2008). *Relations économiques et pressions militaires en Méditerranée orientale et en Libye au temps des pharaons*. Paris: Cybele.

Barnard, H. (2008). *Eastern Desert Ware: Traces of the Inhabitants of the Eastern Deserts in Egypt and Sudan during the 4th–6th Centuries CE*, Oxford: Archaeopress.

Berger-El Naggar, C., Leclant, J., Mathieu, B., and Pierre-Croisiau, I. (2010). *Les Textes de la pyramide de Pépy Ier 1. Description et analyse*, 2nd edn, Cairo: Institut Français d'Archéologie Orientale.

Bestock, L. (2018). *Violence and Power in Ancient Egypt. Image and Ideology before the New Kingdom*. London: Routledge.

Betrò, M. (1996). Punt, la XXVI dinastia e il frammento di statua del Museo Pushkin I.1.B 1025. *Egitto e Vicino Oriente*, 19: 41–49.

Bleckmann, L. E. (2007). *Zur Verräumlichung kollektiver Erinnerungen Landschaften in Preisgedichten der Herero/Himba im Nordwesten*

Namibias. Kölner Ethnologische Beiträge 22 (M. J. Casmir ed.). Cologne: Institut für Völkerkunde, Universität zu Köln.

Bommas, M. (2003). Schrein unter. Gebel es-Silsilah im Neuen Reich. In H. Guksch, E. Hofmann, and M. Bommas, eds., *Grab und Totenkult im Alten Ägypten*, Munich: Verlag C.H. Beck, pp. 88–103.

Bonneau, D. (1964). *La Crue du Nil, divinité égyptienne à travers mille ans d'histoire (332 av.-641 ap. J.-C.)*. Paris: C. Klincksieck.

Boozer, A. L. (2015). The Social Impact of Trade and Migration: The Western Desert in Pharaonic and Post-Pharaonic Egypt. *Oxford Handbooks Online.* DOI: 10.1093/oxfordhb/9780199935413.013.37.

Brémont, A., and Vanhulle, D. (in press). A 'Nubian Touch'? A Rock Art Perspective on Culture Contacts in the First Cataract Area during the Fourth Millennium BCE.

Brown, M. (2015). *Keeping Enemies Closer: Ascribed Material Agency in Ancient Egyptian Rock Inscriptions and the Projection of Presence and Power in Liminal Regions*. Ph.D. Dissertation, Yale University, New Haven.

Brown, M. (2017). Agents of Construction: Ancient Egyptian Rock Inscriptions as Tools of Site Formation and Modern Functional Parallels. *Journal of Egyptian History*, 10:2: 153–211.

Brunner, H. (1937). *Die Texte aus den Gräbern der Herakleopolitenzeit von Siut*. Glückstadt: J. J. Augustin.

Bryan, B.M. (2006). Administration in the Reign of Thutmose III. In E.H. Cline and D. O'Connor, ed., *Thutmose III: A New Biography*. Ann Arbor: University of Michigan Press, pp. 69–122.

Bryan, B. M. (2014). Hatshepsut and Cultic Revelries in the New Kingdom. In J. M. Galán, B. M. Bryan, and P. F. Dorman, eds., *Creativity and Innovation in the Reign of Hatshpesut*, Studies in Ancient Oriental Civilization 69. Chicago: The Oriental Institute, pp. 93–123.

Bubenzer, O. and Bolton, A. (2013). Top down: New Satellite Data and Ground-Truth Data as Base for a Reconstruction of Ancient Caravan Routes. Examples from the Western Desert of Egypt. In F. Förster and H. Riemer, eds., *Desert Road Archaeology in Ancient Egypt and Beyond*. Cologne: Heinrich-Barth-Institut, pp. 61–76.

Butzer, K. and Hansen, C. (1968). *Desert and River in Nubia: Geomorphology and Prehistoric Environments at the Aswan Reservoir*. Madison: University of Wisconsin Press.

Caminos, R. A. (1963a). Papyrus Berlin 10463. *Journal of Egyptian Archaeology*, 49: 29–37.

Caminos, R. A. (1963b). *Gebel es-Silsilah 1: The Shrines*, London: Egypt Exploration Society.

Campagno, M. P. (2013). Late Fourth Millennium BCE. In *UCLA Encyclopedia of Egyptology*, permalink https://escholarship.org/uc/item/9988b193 (accessed 9/2/2019).

Cappers, R. J. T., Sikking, L, Darnell, J. C., and Darnell, D. (2007). Food Supply Along the Theban Desert Roads (Egypt): the Gebel Roma', Wadi el-Hôl, and Gebel Qarn el-Gir Caravansary Deposits. In R. Cappers, ed., *Fields of Change: Progress in African Archaeobotany.* Groningen: Groningen Archaeological Studies 5, pp. 127–138.

Castel, G. and Tallet, P. (2001). Les inscriptions d'El-Harra, oasis de Bahareya. *Bulletin de l'Institut français d'archéologie orientale*, 101: 99–136.

Černý, J. (1956). *Graffiti hiéroglyphiques et hiératiques de la nécropole thébaine. DFIFAO* 9. Cairo: Imprimerie de l'Institut Français d'Archéologie Orientale.

Claassen, C. (2011). Rock Shelters as Women's Retreats: Understanding Newt Kash. *American Antiquity*, 76(4): 628–641.

Clayton, J., de Trafford, A., and Borda, M. (2008). A Hieroglyphic Inscription found at Jebel Uweinat mentioning Yam and Tekhebet. *Sahara*, 19: 129–134.

Clère, J. J. and Vandier, J. (1948). *Textes de la première période intermédiaire et de la Xième Dynastie, Bib. Aeg.* 10. Brussels: Fondation Egyptologique Reine Elisabeth.

Colin, F. (1998). Les Paneia d'El-Buwayb et du Ouadi Minayh sur la piste de Bérénice à Coptos: inscriptions égyptiennes. *Bulletin de l'Institut français d'archéologie orientale*, 98: 89–125.

Colin, F. (2005). Kamose et les Hyksos dans l'oasis de Djesdjes. *Bulletin de l'Institut français d'archéologie orientale*, 105: 35–47.

Cooper, J. and Barnard, H. (2017). New Insights on the Inscription on a Painted Pan-Grave Bucranium, Grave 3252 at Cemetery 3100/3200, Mostagedda (Middle Egypt). *African Archaeological Review*, 34: 363–376.

Cooper, J. (2012). Reconsidering the Location of Yam. *Journal of the American Research Center in Egypt*, 48: 1–21.

Couyat, J. and Montet, P. (1912). *Les Inscriptions hiéroglyphiques et hiératiques du Ouâdi Hammâmât. Cairo: Institut français d'archéologie orientale.*

Crouch, D. (2010). Flirting with Space: Thinking Landscape Relationally. *Cultural Geographies*, 17/1: 5–18.

Dachy, T., Briois, F., Marchand, S., Minotti, M., Lesur, J., and Wuttmann, M. (2018). Living in an Egyptian Oasis: Reconstruction of the Holocene Archaeological Sequence in Kharga. *African Archaeological Review* 35: 531–566.

Darnell, D. (2002). Gravel of the Desert and Broken Pots in the Road: Ceramic Evidence from the Routes between the Nile and Kharga Oasis. In

R. Friedman, ed., *Egypt and Nubia – Gifts of the Desert*, British Museum, London, pp. 156–177.

Darnell, D. and Darnell, J. C. (2013). The Archaeology of Kurkur Oasis, Nuq' Maneih, Bir Nakheila, and the Sinn el-Kaddab. In D. Raue, S. Seidlmayer, and P. Speiser, eds., *The First Cataract of the Nile: one region – diverse perspectives*. Berlin: De Gruyter, pp. 35–52.

Darnell, J. C. (1995). Hathor Returns to Medamûd. *Studien zur Altägyptischen Kultur*, 22: 47–94.

Darnell, J. C. (1999). Pharaonic Rock Inscriptions from HK64 (Chiefly of the Second Intermediate Period and Early New Kingdom. In R. Friedman, et al., Preliminary Report on Field Work at Hierakonpolis: 1996–1998, *Journal of the American Research Center in Egypt*, 36: 1–35.

Darnell, J. C. (2002a). The Narrow Doors of the Desert. In B. David and M. Wilson, eds., *Inscribed Landscapes*, Honolulu: University of Hawaii, pp. 104–121.

Darnell, J. C. (2002b). Opening the Narrow Doors of the Desert: Discoveries of the Theban Desert Road Survey. In R. F. Friedman, ed., *Egypt and Nubia, Gifts of the Desert*, London: British Museum Press, pp. 132–155.

Darnell, J. C. (2003). A Stela of the Reign of Tutankhamun from the Region of Kurkur Oasis. *Studien zur Altägyptischen Kultur*, 31: 73–91.

Darnell, J. C. (2004a). The Route of Eleventh Dynasty Expansion into Nubia, an Interpretation Based on the Rock Inscriptions of Tjehemau at Abisko. *Zeitschrift für ägyptische Sprache und Altertumskunde*, 131: 23–37.

Darnell, J. C. (2004b). Review of Vandekerckhove and Müller-Wollermann, *Die Felsinschriften des Wadi Hilal. Journal of Near Eastern Studies*, 63: 152–155.

Darnell, J. C. (2007). The Deserts. In T. Wilkinson, ed., *The Egyptian World*, London and New York: Routledge, pp. 29–48.

Darnell, J. C. (2008). The Eleventh Dynasty Royal Inscription from Deir el-Ballas. *Revue d'Égyptologie*, 59: 81–106.

Darnell, J. C. (2009). Iconographic Attraction, Iconographic Syntax, and Tableaux of Royal Ritual Power in the Pre- and Proto-Dynastic Rock Inscriptions of the Theban Western Desert. *Archéo-Nil*, 19: 83–107.

Darnell, J. C. (2010a). A Midsummer Night's Succubus – The Herdsman's Encounters in P. Berlin 3024, the Pleasures of Fishing and Fowling, the Songs of the Drinking Place, and the Ancient Egyptian Love Poetry. In S. C. Melville and A. Slotsky, eds., *Opening the Tablet Box, Near Eastern Studies in Honor of Benjamin R. Foster*, Leiden: Brill, pp. 99–140.

Darnell, J. C. (2010b). Opet Festival. In *UCLA Encyclopedia of Egyptology*, retrieved from https://escholarship.org/uc/item/4739r3fr.

Darnell, J. C. (2011). The Wadi of the Horus Qa-a: a Tableau of Royal Ritual Power in the Theban Western Desert. In R. F. Friedman and P. N. Fiske, eds., *Egypt at its Origins 3: Proceedings of the Third International Conference "Origin of the State. Predynastic and Early Dynastic Egypt."* Leuven: Peeters, pp. 1151–1193.

Darnell, J. C. (2013a). *Theban Desert Road Survey II: The Rock Shrine of Pahu, Gebel Akhenaton, and Other Rock Inscriptions from the Western Hinterland of Qamûla*, New Haven: Yale Egyptological Institute.

Darnell, J. C. (2013b). A Bureaucratic Challenge? Archaeology and Administration in a Desert Environment (Second Millennium BCE). In J. C. Moreno Garcia, ed., *Ancient Egyptian Administration*. Leiden: Brill, pp. 785–830.

Darnell, J. C. (2014). The Stela of the Viceroy Usersatet (Boston MFA 25.632), his Shrine at Qasr Ibrim, and the Festival of Nubian Tribute under Amenhotep II. *Égypte Nilotique et Méditerranéenne*, 7: 239–276.

Darnell, J. C. (2017). The Early Hieroglyphic Inscription at el-Khawy. *Archéo-Nil*, 27: 49–64.

Darnell, J. C. (2018). *Homo Pictus* and Painted Men: Depictions and Intimations of Humans in the Rock Art of the Theban Western Desert. In D. Huyge and F. Van Noten, eds., *What Ever Happened to the People? Humans and Anthropomorphs in the Rock Art of Northern Africa*, Brussels: Royal Academy for Overseas Sciences, pp. 397–418.

Darnell, J. C. (2020a). Alchemical Landscapes of Temple and Desert. In C. Geisen, ed., *Ritual Landscape and Performance*. YES 13. New Haven: Yale Egyptology, pp. 121–140.

Darnell, J. C. (2020b). Origins of Writing in Northeastern Africa. In T. Spear, ed., *Oxford Research Encyclopedia of African History*: https://doi.org/10.1093/acrefore/9780190277734.013.594.

Darnell, J. C. (in press a). Dancing Women and Waltzing Ostriches – Ratites in Predynastic and Pharaonic Imagery. In *Festschrift* for Stan Hendrickx.

Darnell, J. C. (in press b). Graffiti, Festivals, and Nubian Self-Presentation – Three Case Studies. In P. Polkowski, ed., *Stone Canvas: Towards a Better Integration of 'Rock Art' and 'Graffiti' Studies in Egypt and Sudan*. Bibliotèque d'Étude, Cairo: Institut Ftançais d'Archéologie Orientale.

Darnell, J. C. (in press c). "Graffiti and Interacting Bodies in the Upper Egyptian Deserts," in C. Ragazzoli and K. Hassan, eds., *Graffiti, Secondary Epigraphy and Rock Inscriptions from Ancient Egypt*. Cairo: Institut Français d'Archéologie Orientale.

Darnell, J. C., with Darnell, D., Hendrickx, S., and Friedman, R. (2002). *The Theban Desert Road Survey in the Egyptian Western Desert I*, Oriental

Institute Publications 119. Chicago: The Oriental Institute of the University of Chicago.

Darnell, J. C., with Darnell, D. (2013). The Girga Road: Abu Ziyar, Tundaba, and the Integration of the Southern Oases into the Pharaonic State. In F. Förster and H. Riemer, eds., *Desert Road Archaeology in Ancient Egypt and Beyond*. Cologne: Heinrich-Barth-Institut, pp. 221–263.

Darnell, J. C. and Darnell, C .M., with Darnell, D. (2016). Umm-Mawagir in Kharga Oasis: An Industrial Landscape of the Late Middle Kingdom/Second Intermediate Period. In G. Miniaci and W. Grajetzki, eds., *The World of Middle Kingdom Egypt (2000-1550 BC)* vol. 2. Middle Kingdom Studies 2. London: Golden House Publications, pp. 27–70.

Darnell, J. C. and Darnell, C. M. (2019). The Late Middle Kingdom and Second Intermediate Period in the 'Southern Oasis' and the Theban Western Desert. In G. E. Bowen and C. A. Hope, eds., *The Oasis Papers 9: A Tribute to Anthony J. Mills after Forty Years in Dakhleh Oasis*. Oxford: Oxbow Books, pp. 165–182.

Darnell, J. C., Darnell, C. M., and Urcia, A. (2018). From Plastic Sheets to Tablet PCs: A Digital Epigraphic Method of Recording Egyptian Rock Art and Inscriptions. *African Archaeological Review*, 35, DOI: 10.1007/s10437-018-9297-z.

Darnell, J. C. and Darnell, C. M., with Urcia, A. (2020). *A Settlement and its Satellites in the Desert Hinterland of Moalla – New Light on Enigmatic Late Roman Sites in the Eastern Desert*. In A. R. Warfe, J. C. R. Gill, et al., eds., *Dust, Demons and Pots: Studies in Honour of Colin A. Hope*. Leuven: Peeters, in press.

Darnell, J. C., and Dobbs-Allsopp, C. *et al.* (2005). *Two Early Alphabetic Inscriptions from the Wadi el-Hol: New Evidence for the Origin of the Alphabet from the Western Desert of Egypt*. Boston: American Schools of Oriental Research.

Darnell, J. C., Hendrickx, S., and Gatto, M. C. (2017). Once more the Nag el-Hamdulab early hieroglyphic annotation. *Archéo-Nil*, 27: 65–74.

Darnell, J. C., Klotz, D., and Manassa, C. (2013). Gods on the Road: The Pantheon of Thebes at Qasr el-Ghueita. In C. Thiers, ed., *Documents de theologies thébaines tardives*. Montpellier: ENiM, pp. 1–31.

Darnell, J. C. and Manassa, C. (2007). *Tutankhamun's Armies: Battle and Conquest in Ancient Egypt's Late 18th Dynasty*. Hoboken: Wiley.

Darnell, J. C. and Manassa, C. (2013). A Trusty Sealbearer on a Mission – the Monuments of Sabastet from the Gebel el-Asr Quarry. In R. Parkinson and H.-W. Fischer-Elfert, eds., *Studies in Honor of Detlef Franke*, Wiesbaden: Harrassowitz, pp. 55–92.

Darnell, J. C. and Vanhulle, D. (f.c.). Setting a Seal Upon the Desert: Protodynastic and Early Dynastic Augmentation and Interpretation of Predynastic Rock Art in the Upper Egyptian Deserts. In M. C. Gatto, *et al.*, eds., *Current Research in the Rock Art of the Eastern* Sahara, *In Memory of Dirk Huyge (1957–2018)*.

Davies, N. de G. (1906). *The Rock Tombs of El Amarna Part IV: Tombs of Penthu, Mahu, and Others*. London, Egypt Exploration Fund.

Davies, N. de G. (1926). *The Tomb of Huy, Viceroy of Nubia in the Reign of Tutankhamun (No. 40)*. London: Egypt Exploration Society.

Davies, W. V. (2017). Nubia in the New Kingdom: the Egyptians at Kurgus. In N. Spencer, A. Stevens, and M. Binder, eds., *Nubia in the New Kingdom: lived experience, pharaonic control and indigenous traditions*. Leuven: Peeters, pp. 65–105.

Dean, C. (1999). *Inka Bodies and the Body of Christ: Corpus Christi in Colonial Cuzco, Peru*. Durham and London: Duke University Press.

Decker, W. (1991). Ägyptischer Sport und Afrika. In D. Mendel and U. Claudi, eds., *Ägypten im afro-orientalischen Kontext: Aufsätze zur Archäologie, Geschichte und Sprache eines unbegrenzten Raumes*. Cologne: Institut für Afrikanistik, Universität zu Köln, pp. 95–108.

Demarée, R. (2002). *Ramesside Ostraca*, London: British Museum Press.

Derchain, P. (1971). *Les monuments religieux à l'entrée de l'ouady Hellal*. Brussels: Fondation Egyptologique Reine Elisabeth.

Desroches-Noblecourt, C. (1995). *Amours et fureurs de la Lointaine, clés pour la comprehension de symboles égyptiens*. Paris: Éditions Stock-Pernoud.

Diego-Espinel, A. (2014). Surveyors, Guides and Other Officials in the Egyptian and Nubian Deserts. *Revue d'Égyptologie*, 65: 29–48.

Dijkstra, J. H. F. (2012). *Philae and the End of Egyptian Religion, A Regional Study of Religious Transformation (298-642 CE)*, OLA 173. Leuven: Peeters.

Dijkstra, J. H. F. (2012). Blemmyes, Noubades and the Eastern Desert in Late Antiquity: Reassessing the Written Sources. In H. Barnard and K. Duistermaat, eds., *The History of the Peoples of the Eastern Desert*, Los Angeles: Cotsen Institute of Archaeology, pp. 239–247.

Dixon, R. (1994). The Unfinished Commonwealth: Boundaries of Civility in Popular Australian Fiction of the First Commonwealth Decade. In C. Tiffin and A. Lawson, eds., *De-Scribing Empire: Post-Colonialism and Textuality*. London and New York: Routledge, pp. 131–140.

Doresse, M. J. (1949). Monastères coptes thébains. *Revue des conferences françaises en Orient* 18(11), 499–512.

Dowson, T. A. (1998). Rain in Bushman Belief, Politics and History: the Rock-Art of Rain-Making in the South-Eastern Mountains, Southern Africa. In

C. Chippendale and P. S. C. Taçon, eds., *The Archaeology of Rock-Art*, Cambridge: Cambridge University Press, pp. 73–89.

Doyen, F., and Gabolde, L. (2017). Egyptians Versus Kushites: The Cultural Question of Writing or Not. In N. Spencer, A. Stevens, and M. Binder, eds., *Nubia in the New Kingdom: Lived Experience, Pharaonic Control and Indigenous Traditions*, British Museum Publications on Egypt and Sudan 3, Leuven, Paris, and Bristol CT: Peeters, pp. 149–158.

Drioton, É. (1939). Une statue prophylactique de Ramses III. *Annales du Service des Antiquités de l'Égypte*, 39: 58–89.

Dunbar, J. H. (1940). *The Rock-Pictures of Lower Nubia*. Cairo: Government Press, Bulâq.

Edwards, D. N. (2004). *The Nubian Past: An Archaeology of the Sudan*. London: Routledge.

Eichler, E. (1993). *Untersuchungen zum Expeditionswesen des ägyptischen Alten Reiches*. Wiesbaden: Harrossowitz.

Engelbach, R. (1939). The Quarries of the Western Nubian Desert and the Ancient Road to Tushka. *Annales du Service des Antiquités de l'Égypte*, 39: 369–390.

Epigraphic Survey (1996). *Reliefs and Inscriptions at Luxor Temple 1: The Festival Procession of Opet in the Colonnade Hall*. OIP 112. Chicago: Oriental Institute.

Espinel, A. D. (2005). A Newly Identified Stela from Wadi el-Hudi. *Journal of Egyptian Archaeology*, 91: 65–66.

Fakhry, A. (1940). Wâdi-el-Natrûn. *Annales du Service des Antiquités de l'Égypte*, 40: 837–848.

Faraji, S. (2011). Kush and Rome on the Egyptian Southern Frontier: Where Barbarians Worshipped as Romans and Romans Worshipped as Barbarians. In R. W. Mathisen and D. Shanzer, eds., *Romans, Barbarians, and the Transformation of the Roman World: Cultural Interaction and the Creation of Identity in Late Antiquity*, Farnham: Ashgate, pp. 228–231.

Finnestad, R. B. (1997). Temples of the Ptolemaic and Roman Periods: Ancient Traditions in New Contexts. In B. E. Shafer, ed., *Temples of Ancient Egypt*, Ithaca: Cornell University Press, pp. 185–237.

Fischer-Elfert, H.-W. (1998). *Die Vision von der Statue im Stein*, Heidelberg: Universitätsverlag C. Winter.

Fleming, J. (2001). *Graffiti and the Writing Arts of Early Modern England*, London: Reaktion Books Ltd.

Förster, F. (2015). *Der Abu Ballas-Weg. Eine pharaonische Karawanenroute durch die Libysche Wüste*, Cologne: Heinrich-Barth-Institut.

Förster, F., Riemer, H., and Kuper, R. (2012). The Cave of the Beasts (Gilf Kebir, SW Egypt) and it chronological and cultural affiliation. In D. Huyge, et al., eds. *Chronological and Palaeoenvironmental Issues in the Rock Art of Northern Africa*. Brussels: Royal Academy of Overseas Sciences, pp. 197–216.

Fowler, C. (2008). Landscape and Personhood. In B. David and J. Thomas, eds., *Handbook of Landscape Archaeology*, Walnut Creek, CA: Left Coast Press, pp. 291–299.

Franke, D. (1994). *Das Heiligtum des Heqaib auf Elephantine*, Heidelberg: Heidelberger Orientverlag.

Franke, D. (2003). Sem-Priest on Duty. In S. Quirke, ed., *Discovering Egypt from the Neva, The Egyptological Legacy of Oleg D Berlev*, Berlin: Achet-Verlag, pp. 73–75.

Franzmeier, H. (2010). *Ein Brunnen in der Ramses-Stadt: Zur Typologie und Funktion von Brunnen und Zisternen im pharaonischen Ägypten*. Hildesheim: Verlag Gebrüder Gerstenberg.

Friedman, R. (1999). Excavations at HK64. In R. Friedman, et al., Preliminary Report on Field Work at Hierakonpolis: 1996-1998, *Journal of the American Research Center in Egypt*, 36: 1–35.

Friedman, R., *et al*. (2018). Natural Mummies from Predynastic Egypt Reveal the World's Earliest Figural Tattoos. *Journal of Archaeological Science*, 92: 116–125.

Gabolde, M. (2015). *Toutankhamon*. Paris: Pygmalion.

Garbrecht, G. and Bertram, H.-U. (1983). *Der Sadd el-Kafara: die älteste Talsperre der Welt (2600 v. Chr.)*. 2 vols. Braunschweig: Leichtweiss-Institut für Wasserbau der Technischen Universität Braunschweig.

Gardiner, A. H., Peet, T. E., and Černý, J. (1952). *The Inscriptions of Sinai*, Part 1, London: Egypt Exploration Society.

Gasperini, V. and Pethen, H. (2018). Roads from Baharia to Faiyum: A Study in Remotely Sensed Data. *Ägypten und Levante*, 28: 181–197.

Gasse, A. (2016). Wadi Hammamat on the Road to Punt. *Abgadiyat*, 11: 44–50.

Gasse, A. and Rondot, V. (2007). *Les inscriptions de Séhel, MIFAO* 126. Cairo: Institut Français d'Archéologie Orientale.

Gatto, M. C. (2013). Beyond the Shale: Pottery and Cultures in the Prehistory of the Egyptian Western Desert. In R. S. Bagnall, P. Davoli, and C. A. Hope. eds., *The Oasis Papers 6: Proceedings of the Sixth International Conference of the Dakhleh Oasis Project, Lecce, September 2009*. Oxford: Oxbow Books, 61–72.

Gerke, S. (2014). *Der altägyptische Greif: von der Vielfalt eines "Fabeltiers."* Hamburg: Helmut Buske.

Giddy, L. (1987). *Egyptian Oases*. Warminster: Aris & Phillips.

Gill, J. C. R. (2016). *Dakhleh Oasis and the Western Desert of Egypt under the Ptolemies*. Oxford: Oxbow Books.

Gleichen, [E.], Lt.-Col. Count, ed. (1905). *The Anglo-Egyptian Sudan: A Compendium Prepared by Officers of the Sudan Government*. London: His Majesty's Printing Office.

Goldwasser, O. (2006). Canaanites Reading Hieroglyphs, Horus is Hathor? – The Invention of the Alphabet in Sinai. *Ägypten und Levante*, 9: 121–160.

González-Tablas Nieto, J. (2014). Quarrying Beautiful Bekhen Stone for the Pharaoh: the Exploitation of Wadi Hammamat in the Reign of Amenemhat III. *Journal of Egyptian History*, 7 (1): 34–66.

Graff, G. (2009). *Les peintures sur vases de Nagada I-Nagada II, nouvelle approche sémiologique de l'iconographie prédynastique*. Leuven: Leuven University Press.

Graff, G., Eyckerman, M., and Hendrickx, S. (2011). Architectural Elements on Decorated Pottery and the Ritual Presentation of Desert Animals. In R. Friedman and P. Fiske, eds., *Egypt at its Origins 3, Proceedings of the Third International Conference "Origin of the State. Predynastic and Early Dynastic Egypt."* Leuven: Peeters, pp. 437–465.

Gratien, B. (2004). Les fonctionnaires des sites égyptiens de Nubie au Moyen Empire, correspondance entre inscriptions rupestres et documents sigillaires. In A. Gasse and V. Rondot, eds., *Séhel entre Égypte et Nubie: Inscriptions rupestres et graffiti de l'époque pharaonique*. Montpellier: Univeristé Paul Valery, pp. 161–174.

Habachi, L. (1973). The Two Rock-Stelae of Sethos I in the Cataract Area Speaking of Huge Statues and Obelisks. *Bulletin de l'Institut français d'archéologie orientale*, 73: 113–125.

Habachi, L. (1982). *The Second Stela of Kamose, and his Struggle against the Hyksos Ruler and his Capital*. Glückstadt, J. J. Augustin.

Hamilton, C. (2016). Enlightening the Enduring Engravings: The Expeditions of Raneb. *Archéo-Nil*, 26: 185–204.

Hamilton, C. (2019). Mapping Evidence for Early Dynastic Activity in the Dakhleh Region. In G. E. Bowden and C. A. Hope, eds., *The Oasis Papers 9*. Oxford: Oxbow Books, pp. 143–170.

Hamilton, G. (2006). *The Origins of the West Semitic Alphabet in Egyptian Scripts*. Washington, D.C.: Catholic Bible Association of America.

Hannig, R. (2006). *Ägyptisches Wøurterbuch II Mittleres Reich und Zweite Zwischenzeit 1*, Mainz am Rhein: Verlag Philipp von Zabern.

Harrell, J. A. (2002). Pharaonic Stone Quarries in the Egyptian Deserts. In R. F. Friedman, ed., *Egypt and Nubia: Gifts of the Desert*. London: British Museum Press, pp. 232–243.

Harrell, J. A. and Brown, V. M. (1992). The Oldest Surviving Topographical Map from Ancient Egypt (Turin Papyri 1879, 1899, and 1969). *Journal of the American Research Center in Egypt*, 29: 81–105.

Hassanein Bey, A. M. (1925). *The Lost Oases*. New York and London: The Century Co.

Hays-Gilpin, K. A. (2004). *Ambiguous Images: Gender and Rock Art*. Gender and Archaeology Series 7, Walnut Creek, CA: AltaMira Press.

Hendrickx, S. (2002). Bovines in Egyptian Predynastic and Early Dynastic Iconography. In F. A. Hassan, ed., *Droughts, Food and Culture. Ecological Change and Foor Security in Africa's Later Prehistory*. New York: Kluwer Academic, pp. 275–318.

Hendrickx, S. (2006). The Dog, the *Lycaon pictus* and Order over Chaos in Predynastic Egypt. In K. Kroeper, M. Chłodnicki, and M. Kobusiewicz, eds., *Archaeology of Early Northeastern Africa. In Memory of Lech Krzyaniak*. Poznán: Poznán Archaeological Museum, pp. 723–749.

Hendrickx, S. and Eyckerman, M. (2012). Visual Representation and State Development in Egypt. *Archéo-Nil* 22: 23–72.

Hendrickx, S, Riemer, H., Förster, F., and Darnell, J. C. (2010). Late Predynastic/ Early Dynastic Rock Art Scenes of Barbary Sheep Hunting from Egypt's Western Desert. From Capturing Wild Animals to the 'Women of the Acacia House.' In H. Riemer, F. Förster, M. Herb, and N. Pöllath, eds., *Desert Animals in the Eastern Sahara: Status, Economic Significance and Cultural Reflection in Antiquity*. Cologne: Heinrich Barth Institut, pp. 189–244.

Hendrickx, S., *et al.* (2014-15). The Origin and Early Significance of the White Crown. *Mitteilungen des Deutschen Archäologischen Instituts Abteilung Kairo*, 70–71: 227–238.

Herbin, F. R. (1994). *Le livre de parcourir l'éternité*. Leuven: Peeters.

Hikade, T. (2001). *Das Expeditionswesen im ägyptischen Neuen Reich. Ein Beitrag zu Rohstoffversorgung und Außenhandel*. Heidelberg: Heidelberger Orientverlag.

Hintze, F. and Reineke, W. F. (1989). *Felsinschriften aus dem sudanesischen Nubien*, Vol. 1, Publikation der Nubien-Expedition 1961–1963. Berlin: Akademie Verlag.

Hölzl, R. (2002). *Ägyptische Opfertafeln und Kultbecken*. Hildesheim: Gerstenberg Verlag.

Hoffmeier, J. K. (2013). Reconstructing Egypt's Eastern Frontier Defense Network in the New Kingdom (Late Bronze Age). In F. Jesse and C. Vogel, eds., *The Power of Walls – Fortifications in Ancient Northeastern Africa*. Cologne: Heinrich-Barth-Institut, pp. 163–194.

Hoffmeier, J. K. and Moshier, S. O. (2013). "A Highway out of Egypt": The Main Road from Egypt to Canaan. In F. Förster and H. Riemer, eds., *Desert Road Archaeology in Ancient Egypt and Beyond*. Cologne: Heinrich-Barth-Institut, pp. 485–510.

Hope, C. (1980). Dakhleh Oasis Project – Report on the Study of the Pottery and Kilns. *Journal of the Society for the Study of Egyptian Antiquities*, 10: 283–313.

Hope, C. (1983). Dakhleh Oasis Project – Preliminary Report on the Study of the Pottery – Fifth Season. *Journal of the Society for the Study of Egyptian Antiquities*, 13: 142–157.

Hope, C. A. and Kaper, O. E. (2010). A Governor of Dakhleh Oasis in the Early Middle Kingdom. In A. Woods, A. McFarlane, and S. Binder, eds., *Egyptian Culture and Society. Studies in Honour of Naguib Kanawati*, vol. 1. Cairo: Conseil suprême des antiquités, pp. 219–245.

Hope, C. A. and Pettman, A. (2014). Egyptian Connections with Dakhleh Oasis in the Early Dynastic Period to Dynasty IV: new data from Mut al-Kharab. In R. S. Bagnall, P. Davoli, and C. A. Hope, eds., *The Oasis Papers 6: Proceedings of the Sixth International Conference of the Dakhleh Oasis Project*. Oxford: Oxbow Books, pp. 147–166.

Hope, C. A., Pettman, A., and Warfe, A. R. (2019). The Egyptian Annexation of Dakhleh Oasis: New Evidence from Mut-al Kharab. In K. O. Kuraszkiewicz, E. Köpp, and D. Takács, eds., *'The Perfection That Endures . . . ': Studies on Old Kingdom Art and Archaeology*. Warsaw: Department of Egyptology, University of Warsaw, pp. 191–207.

Horn, M. (2017). Re-appraising the Tasian-Badarian Divide in the Qau-Matmar Region: A Critical Review of Cultural Proxies and a Comparative Analysis of Burial Dress. In B. Midant-Reynes and Y. Tristan, with E. M. Ryan, eds., *Egypt at Its Origins* 5, OLA 260. Leuven, Paris, and Bristol CT, Peeters, pp. 337–377.

Hubschmann, C. (2019). Dakhleh Oasis in the Late Period. In G. E. Bowen and C. A. Hope, eds., *The Oasis Papers 9: A Tribute to Anthony J. Mills after Forty Years in Dakhleh Oasis*. Oxford: Oxbow Books, pp. 265–276.

Hulin, L. (2015). Marsa Matruh Revisited: Modelling Interaction at a Late Bronze Age Harbour on the Egyptian Coast. Retrieved from https://ora .ox.ac.uk/objects/uuid:8ba7caca-71c3-446e-b9db-faa9ab51e182.

Hussein, H. and Alim, E. A. (2015). The Way(s) of Horus in the Saite Period: Tell el-Kedwa and its Key Location Guarding Egypt's Northeastern Frontier. *Journal of Ancient Egyptian Interconnections*, 7(1): 39–51.

Huyge, D. (1998). Late Palaeolithic and Epipaleolithic rock are in Egypt: Qurta and El-Hosh, *Archéo-Nil*, 19: 108–120.

Huyge, D. (2002). Cosmology, Ideology, and Personal Religious Practice in Ancient Egyptian Rock Art. In R. Friedman, ed., *Egypt and Nubia. Gifts of the Desert*, London: British Museum, pp. 192–206.

Huyge, D. (2003). Grandeur in Confined Spaces: Current Rock Art Research in Egypt. In P. G. Bahn and A. Fossati, eds., *Rock Art Studies: News of the World 2. Developments in Rock Art Research 1995–1999*. Oxford: Oxbow Books, pp. 59–73.

Huyge, D. (2013). 10.000 ans avant 'L'Art du contour.' In Delvaux, L, Huyge, D., Pierlot, A., *et al.*, eds., *Regards sur le dessin égyptien*. Brussels: Musées royaux d'Art et d'Histoire, pp. 12–23.

Huyge, D. and Claes, W. (2012). El-Hosh et Qurta: sur les traces du plus ancien art égyptien. In Bavay, L. et al., eds., *Ceci n'est pas une pyramide ... Un siècle de recherche archéologique belge en Égypte*. Leuven: Peeters, pp. 32–45.

Ikram, S. and Rossi, C. (2004). An Early Dynastic *Serekh* from the Kharga Oasis. *Journal of Egyptian Archaeology*, 90: 211–214.

Jacquet-Gordon, H. (2003). *The Graffiti on the Khonsu Temple Roof at Karnak: A Manifestation of Personal Piety*. Chicago: The Oriental Institute of the University of Chicago.

Jacquet, J. (1967). Observations sur l'evolution architecturale des temples rupestres. In *Nubie par divers archéologues et historiens*. Cairo: Cahiers d'Histoire Égyptienne, pp. 69–91.

Jäger, S. (2004). *Altägyptische Berufstypologien*. Göttingen: Seminar für Ägyptologie und Koptologie.

Janssen, J. (2004). *Grain Transport in the Ramesside Period: Papyrus Baldwin (BM EA 10061) and Papyrus Amiens*. London: British Museum Press.

Jaritz, H. (1981). Zum Heiligtum am Gebel Tingar. *Mitteilungen des Deutschen Archäologischen Instituts, Abteilung Kairo*, 37: 241–246.

Jesse, F. (2019). Fending off the Desert Dwellers – The Gala Abu Ahmed Fortress and other fortified Places in the South Libyan Desert. In D. Raue, ed., *Handbook of Ancient Nubia*, Volume 2. Berlin: De Gruyter, pp. 1069–1091.

Jeuthe, C. (2018). The Governor's Palaces at Ayn Asil/Balat (Dakhla Oasis/ Western Desert). In M. Bietak and S. Prell, eds., *Ancient Egyptian and Ancient Near Eastern Palaces*, Volume 1. Vienna: Austrian Academy of Sciences, pp. 125–40.

Jeuthe, C., Le Provost, V., and Soukiassian, G. (2013). Ayn Asil, palais des gouverneurs du règne de Pépy II: état des recherches sur la partie sud. *Bulletin de l'Institut Français d'Archéologie Orientale*, 113: 203–238.

Judd, T. (2009). *Rock art of the Eastern Desert of Egypt: Content, Comparisons, Dating and Significance*. Oxford: Archaeopress.

Kaper, O. and Willems, H. (2002). Policing the Desert: Old Kingdom Activity around the Dakhleh Oasis. In R. Friedman, ed., *Egypt and Nubia – Gifts of the Desert*. London: British Museum Press, pp. 79–94.

Kaper, O. (2012). The Western Oases. In C. Riggs, ed., *The Oxford Handbook of Roman Egypt*. Oxford: Oxford University Press, pp. 717–735.

Kaper, O. (2015). A Stela of Amenemhet IV from the Main Temple at Berenike. *Bibliotheca Orientalis*, LXXII (5/6): 585–602.

Keimer, L. (1944). L'horreur des égyptiens pour les demons du desert. *Bulletin de l'Institut d'Égypte* 26: 135–147.

Kemp, B. J. (2006). *Ancient Egypt: Anatomy of a Civilisation*. London: Routledge.

Kitchen, K. A. (1975). *Ramesside Inscriptions Vol. 1: Historical and Biographical*, Oxford: B. H. Blackwell Ltd.

Kitchen, K. A. (1979). *Ramesside Inscriptions. Vol. 2: Historical and Biographical*, Oxford: B. H. Blackwell Ltd.

Klemm, R. and Klemm, D. (2008). *Stones and Quarries in Ancient Egypt*. London: British Museum Press.

Klotz, D. (2013). Administration of the Deserts and Oases: First Millennium BCE. In J. C. Moreno Garcia, ed., *Ancient Egyptian Administration*. Leiden: Brill, pp. 901–909.

Klotz, D. (2015). Darius I and the Sabaeans: Ancient Partners in Red Sea Navigation. *Journal of Near Eastern Studies*, 74: 267–280.

Klotz, D. and Brown, M. (2017). The Enigmatic Statuette of Djehutymose (MFA 24.743): Deputy of Wawat and Viceroy of Kush. *Journal of the American Research Center in Egypt*, 52: 269–302.

Köpp, H. (2013). Desert Travel and Transport in Ancient Egypt. An Overview based on Epigraphic, Pictorial and Archaeological Evidence. In F. Förster and H. Riemer, eds., *Desert Road Archaeology in Ancient Egypt and Beyond*. Cologne: Heinrich-Barth-Institut, pp. 107–132.

Knoblauch, C. (2019). Middle Kingdom Fortresses. In D. Raue, ed., *Handbook of Ancient Nubia*. Boston: De Gruyters, pp. 367–391.

Köpp-Junk, H., Riemer, H., and Förster, F. (2017). Mobility in Ancient Egypt – Roads and Travel in the Nile Valley and Adjacent Deserts. In S. Scharl and B. Gehlen, eds., *Mobility in Prehistoric Sedentary Societies*. Rahden: Verlag Marie Leidorf, pp. 277–300.

Kraemer, B. and Liszka, K. (2016). Evidence for Administration of the Nubian Fortresses in the Late Middle Kingdom: The Semna Dispatches. *Journal of Egyptian History*, 9: 1–65.

Krzywinski, K. (2012). The Eastern Desert Tombs and Cultural Continuity. In H. Barnard and K. Duistermaat, eds., *The History of the Peoples of the Eastern Desert*. Los Angeles: Cotsen Institute of Archaeology, pp. 140–155.

Kubisch, S. (2018). *Lebensbilder der 2. Zwischenzeit. Biographische Inscriften der 13.-17. Dynastie*. Berlin: Walter De Gruyter.

Kuper, R., *et al.* (2013). *Wadi Sura – The Cave of Beasts, A Rock Art Site in the Gilf Kebir (SW-Egypt)*. Cologne: Heinrich-Barth-Institut.

Kuraszkiewicz, K. O. (2006). The title *xtmtj nTr* – God's Sealer – in the Old Kingdom. In M. Bárta, ed., *The Old Kingdom Art and Archaeology, Proceedings of the Conference Helf in Prague, May 31-June 4, 2004*. Prague: Czech Institute of Egyptology, pp. 193–202.

Kuznar, L. A. and Sedlmeyer, R. (2008). Nomad: an Agent-Based Model (ABM) of Pastoralist-Agriculturalist Interaction. In H. Barnard and W. Wendrich, eds., *The Archaeology of Mobility: Old World and New World Nomadism*, Los Angeles: Cotsen Institute of Archaeology, pp. 557–583.

Lankester, F. (2013). *Desert Boats: Predynastic and Pharaonic Era Rock-Art in Egypt's Central Eastern Desert: Distribution, Dating and Interpretation*. Oxford: Archaeopress.

Lassányi, G. (2010). Test–Excavations in the Settlement. In U. Luft, ed., *Bi'r Minayh, Report on the Survey 1998–2004*. Budapest: Archaeolingua Alapítvány, pp. 255–257.

Lassányi, G. (2012). On the Archaeology of the Native Population of the Eastern Desert in the First-Seventh Centuries CE. In H. Barnard and K. Duistermaat, eds., *The History of the Peoples of the Eastern Desert*. Los Angeles: Cotsen Institute of Archaeology, pp. 248–269.

Lazaridis, N. (2019). Desert Deviations: Massaging Standard Writing Conventions in North Kharga's Ancient Graffiti. In G. E. Bowden and C. A. Hope, eds., *The Oasis Papers 9*. Oxford: Oxbow Books, pp. 127–134.

Le Provost, V. (2016). À propos de céramiques à décor de sauriens: Ayn Asil (oasis Dakhla) fin IIIe/début IIe millénaire. *Bulletin de liaison de la céramique égyptienne*, 26: 229–249.

Leblanc, C. (1989). *Ta Set Neferou. Une nécropole de Thebes-Ouest et son histoire. I: Géographie – toponymie, historique de l'exploration scientifique du site*. Cairo: Nubar Printing House.

Leitz, C. *et al.*, eds. (2002). *Lexikon der ägyptischen Götter und Götterbezeichnungen*, Volume V. Leuven: Peeters.

Leprohon, R. J. (1978). The Personnel of the Middle Kingdom Funerary Stelae. *Journal of the American Research Center in Egypt*, 15: 33–38.

von Lieven, A. (2013). Von Göttern und Gesteinen. *Zeitschrift für ägyptische Sprache und Altertumskunde*, 140: 24–35.

Liszka, K. (2015). Are the Bearers of the Pan-Grave Archaeological Culture Identical to the Medjay People in the Egyptian Textual Record? *Journal of Ancient Egyptian Interconnections*, 7: 42–60.

Liszka, K. (2010). 'Medjay' (no. 188) in the Onomasticon of Amenemope. In Z. Hawass and J. H. Wegner, eds., *Millions of Jubilees, Studies in Honor of David P. Silverman*. Cairo: Publications du Conseil Suprême des Antiquités de l'Égypte, pp. 315–331.

Liverani, M. (2000). The Libyan Caravan Road in Herodotus IV.181-185. *Journal of the Economic and Social History of the Orient*, 43 (4): 496–520.

Lohwasser, A. (2013). Tracks in the Bayuda desert. The project 'Wadi Abu Dom Itinerary' (W.A.D.I.). In F. Förster and H. Riemer, eds., *Desert Road Archaeology in Ancient Egypt and Beyond*. Cologne: Heinrich-Barth-Institut, pp. 425–435.

Lovata, T. (2015). Marked Trees: Exploring the Context of Southern Rocky Mountain Arborglyphs. In T. Lovata and E. Olton, eds., *Understanding Graffiti: Multidisciplinary Studies from Prehistory to the Present*, Walnut Creek, CA: Left Coast Press, pp. 91–104.

Luiselli, M. M. (2011). *Die Suche nach Gottesnähe, Untersuchungen zur Persönlichen Frömmigkeit in Ägypten von der Ersten Zwischenzeit bis zum Ende des Neuen Reiches*. Wiesbaden: Harrossowitz Verlag.

Lull, J. (2006). *Los sumos sacerdotes de Amón tebanos de la wHm mswt y dinistía XXI (ca. 1083-945 a.C.)*. Oxford: Archaeopress.

Mahfouz, E.-S. (2005). Les Directeurs des Déserts Aurifères D'Amon. *Revue d'égyptologie*, 56: 55–78.

Mairs, R. (2011). Egyptian 'Inscriptions' and Greek 'Graffiti' at El Kanais in the Egyptian Eastern Desert. In J. A. Baird and C. Taylor, eds., *Ancient Graffiti in Context*, New York: Routledge, pp. 153–164.

Manassa, C. (2003). *The Great Karnak Inscription of Merneptah: Grand Strategy in the 13th Century BC*. New Haven: Yale Egyptological Seminar.

Marchand, S. and Tallet, P. (1999). Ayn Asil et l'oasis de Dakhla au Nouvel Empire. *Bulletin de l'Institut Français d'Archéologie Orientale*, 99: 307–352.

Marchand, S. and Soukiassian, G. (2010). *Balat VIII: un habitat de la XIIIe dynastie – 2e Période Intermédiaire à Ayn Asil*. Cairo: Institut Français d'Archéologie Orientale,

Marée, M. (2009). The 12th – 17th Dynasties at Gebel el-Zeit: A Closer Look at the Inscribed Royal Material. *Bibliotheca Orientalis*, 66 (3–4): 147–162.

Marochetti, E. F. (2010). *The Reliefs of the Chapel of Nebhepetre Mentuhotep at Gebelein (CGT 7003/1-277)*. Leiden: Brill.

Martin, E. F. (2005). *The Architecture of Imperialism: military bases and the evolution of foreign policy in Egypt's New Kingdom*. Leiden: Brill.

Meeks, D. (1991). Oiseaux des carrieres et des caverns. In U. Verhoeven and E. Graefe, eds., *Religion und Philosophie im Alten Ägypten*. Leuven: Peeters, pp. 233–241.

Moeller, N. (2016). *The Archaeology of Urbanism in Ancient Egypt, From the Predynastic Period to the End of the Middle Kingdom*. Cambridge: Cambridge University Press.

Monnier, F. (2010). *Les forteresses égyptiennes, Du Prédynastique au Nouvel Empire*. Brussels: Éditions Safran.

Morel, V. (2021). Écrire en contexte expéditionnaire. Une enquête interprétative sur les inscriptions des carriéres du ouadi Hammamat, de l'Ancien à la fin du Moyen Empire. unpublished PhD dissertation, University of Geneva and École Pratique des Hautes Études.

Moreno Garcia, J. C. (1999). *Hwt et le milieu rural égyptien du IIIe millenaire: économie, administration et organization territorial*. Paris: H. Champion.

Moreno Garcia, J. C. (2010). War in Old Kingdom Egypt (2686–2125 BCE). In J. Vidal, ed., *Studies on War in the Ancient Near East. Collected Essays on Military History*. Münster: Ugarit Verlag, pp. 5–41.

Moreno Garcia, J. C. (2013). The Territorial Administration of the Kingdom in the 3rd Millennium. In J. C. Moreno Garcia, ed., *Ancient Egyptian Administration*. Leiden: Brill, pp. 85–151.

Moreno Garcia, J. C. (2017). Trade and Power in Ancient Egypt: Middle Egypt in the Late Third/Early Second Millennium BC." *Journal of Archaeological Research*, 252: 87–132.

Moreno Garcia, J. C. (2018). Elusive "Libyans": Identities, Lifestyles and Mobile Populations in NE Africa (late 4th – early 2nd millennium BCE). *Journal of Egyptian History*, 11: 147–184.

Morris, E.F. (2005). *The Architecture of Imperialism: Military Bases and the Evolution of Foreign Policy in Egypt's New Kingdom*. Leiden, Boston: Brill.

Mostafa, M. F. (2014). *The Mastaba of ¥mAj at Nag' Kom el-Koffar, Qift*. Cairo: Ministry of Antiquities and Heritage.

Moussa, A. (1981). A Stela of Taharqa from the Desert Road at Dashur. *MDAIK*, 37: 331–334.

Morrow, M., *et al.* (2010). *Desert RATS: Rock Art Topographical Survey in Egypt's Eastern Desert: Site Catalogue*. Oxford: Archaeopress.

Müller, S. (2016). Kambyses II., Alexander und Siwa: die ökonomisch-geopolitische Dimension. In C. Binder, H. Börm, and A. Luther, eds.,

Diwan: studies in the history and culture of the ancient Near East and the eastern Mediterranean. Duisburg: Wellem, pp. 223–245.

Murray, G. W. (1939). The Road to Chephren's quarries. *The Geographical Journal*, 94/2: 97–114.

Newton, C., Whitbread, T., Agut-Labordère, D., and Wuttman, M. (2013). L'Agriculture Oasienne à l'Époque Perse dans le Sud de l'Oasis de Kharga (Égypte, Ve-IVe s. AEC). *Revue d'Ethnoécologie*, 4: 2–18.

Nyord, R. (2020). *Seeing Perfection: Ancient Egyptian Images beyond Representation*. Cambridge: Cambridge University Press.

O'Connor, D. (1986). The Locations of Yam and Kush and their Historical Implications. *Journal of the American Research Center in Egypt*, 23: 27–50.

O'Connor, D. (2009). *Abydos: Egypt's First Pharaohs and the Cult of Osiris*. London: Thames & Hudson.

O'Connor, D. (2014). *The Old Kingdom Town of Buhen*. London: Egypt Exploration Society.

Olette-Pelletier, J.-G., f.c. *Min,"l'Horus victorieux"*. *Le dieu Min au Moyen Empire, Homo Religiosus* 21.

Pantalacci, L. (2013a). Balat, a Frontier Town and its Archive. In J. C. Moreno Garcia, ed., *Ancient Egyptian Administration*. Leiden: Brill, pp. 197–214.

Pantalacci, L. (2013b). Broadening Horizons: Distant Places and Travels in Dakhla and the Western Desert at the End of the 3rd Millennium. In F. Förster and H. Riemer, eds., *Desert Road Archaeology in Ancient Egypt and Beyond*. Cologne: Heinrich-Barth-Institut, pp. 283–296.

Parkinson, R. B. (2002). *Poetry and Culture in Middle Kingdom Egypt: a Dark Side to Perfection*, London and New York: Continuum.

Parkinson, R. B. and Schofield, L. (1995). Images of Mycenaeans: A Recently Acquired Painted Papyrus from el-Amarna. In W. V. Davies and L. Schofield, eds., *Egypt, the Aegean and the Levant: Interconnections in the second millennium BC*. London: British Museum Press, pp. 125–126.

Patch, D. C., ed. (2011). *Dawn of Egyptian Art*, New York: Metropolitan Museum of Art.

Peden, A. J. (2001). *The Graffiti of Pharaonic Egypt*, PdÄ 17, Leiden: Brill.

Pethen, H. (2014). The Pharaoh as Horus: Three Dimensional Figurines from Mining Sites and the Religious Context for the Extraction of Minerals in the Middle Kingdom. In T. Lekov and E. Buzov, eds., *Cult and Belief in Ancient Egypt: Proceedings of the Fourth International Congress for Young Egyptologists*. Sofia: East West, pp. 151–162.

Pethen, H. (2017). The Stelae Ridge Cairns: A Reassessment of the Archaeological Evidence. In G. Rosati and M. C. Guidotti, eds.,

Proceedings of the XI International Congress of Egyptologists. Oxford: Archaeopress Publishing, pp. 485–490.

Petrie, W. M. F. (1906). *Reseaches in Sinai.* London: J. Murray.

Pierce, R. H. (2012). A Blemmy by Any Other Name ... A Study in Greek Ethnography. In H. Barnard and K. Duistermaat, eds., *The History of the Peoples of the Eastern Desert*, Los Angeles: Cotsen Institute of Archaeology, pp. 227–237.

Pinch, G. (1993). *Votive Offerings to Hathor*, Oxford: Griffith Institute.

Plesch, V. (2015). Beyond Art History: Graffiti on Frescoes. In T. Lovata and E. Olton, eds., *Understanding Graffiti*. Walnut Creek: Left Coast Press, pp. 47–57.

Polkowski, P. L. (2018). Feet, Sandals and Animate Landscapes. Some Considerations on the Rock Art of Dakhleh Oasis, Egypt. In D. Huyge and F. Van Noten, eds., *What Ever Happened to the People? Humans and Anthropomorphs in the Rock Art of Northern Africa.* Brussels: Royal Academy for Overseas Sciences, pp. 371–395.

Polkowski, P. L. (2019). Seth on Rocks: Rock Art Imagery in Dakhleh Oasis of the Pharaonic Period. In G. E. Bowden and C. A. Hope, eds., *The Oasis Papers 9*. Oxford: Oxbow Books, pp. 143–170.

Polz, D. (2018). The Territorial Claim and the Political Role of the Theban State at the End of the Second Intermediate Period: A Case Study. In I. Forstner-Müller and N. Moeller, eds., *The Hyksos Ruler Khyan and the Early Second Intermediate Period in Egypt: Problems and Priorities of Current Research.* Vienna: Österreichisches Archäologisches Institut, pp. 210–234.

Poon, K. W. C. and Quickenden, T. I. (2006). A Review of Tattooing in Ancient Egypt. *Bulletin of the Australian Centre for Egyptology*, 17: 123–136.

Preisigke, F. and Spiegelberg, W. (1915). *Ägyptische und griechische Inschriften und Graffiti aus den Steinbrüchen der Gebel Silsile (Oberägypten)*, Strassburg: Trübner.

Quack, F. (2010). The Animals of the Desert and the Return of the Goddess. In H. Riemer, F. Förster, M. Herb, and N. Pöllath, eds., *Desert Animals in the Eastern Sahara: Status, Economic Significance and Cultural Reflection in Antiquity*, Cologne: Heinrich Barth Institut, pp. 341–361.

Quirke, S. (1989). Frontier or Border? The Northeast Delta in Middle Kingdom Texts. In *The Archaeology, Geography and History of the Egyptian Delta in Pharaonic Times*. Oxford: Discussions in Egyptology, pp. 261–274.

Ragazzoli, C. (2017). *La grotte des scribes à Deir el-Bahari: la tombe MMA 504 et ses graffiti*, Cairo: Institut français d'archéologie orientale du Caire.

Rainbird, P. (2008). The Body and the Senses: Implications for Landscape Archaeology. In B. David and J. Thomas, eds., *Handbook of Landscape Archaeology*, Walnut Creek, CA: Left Coast Press Inc., pp. 263–270.

Raue, D. (2019). Nubians in Egypt in the 3rd and 2nd Millennium BC. In D. Raue, ed., *Handbook of Ancient Nubia*, Volume 1. Berlin: De Gruyter, pp. 567–588.

Régen, I., and Soukiassian, G. (2008). *Gebel el-Zeit II. La matériel inscrit.* Cairo: Institut Français d'Archéologie Orientale.

Richardson, S. (1999). Libya domestica: Libyan Trade and Society on the Eve of the Invasions of Egypt. *Journal of the American Research Center in Egypt*, 36: 149–164.

Riemer, H. (2007). When Hunters Started Herding: Pastro-Foragers and the Complexity of Holocene Economic Change in the Western Desert of Egypt. In M. Bollig, O. Bubenezer, R. Vogelsang, and H.-P. Wotzka, eds., *Aridity, Change and Conflict in Africa*, Colloquium Africanum 2. Cologne: Heinrich-Barth-Institut, pp. 105–144.

Riemer, H. (2011). *El Kharafish. The Archaeology of Sheikh Muftah Pastoral Nomads in the Desert around Dakhla* Oasis *(Egypt)*. CologneL Heinrich-Barth-Institut.

Riemer, H. and Förster, F. (2013). Ancient Desert Roads: Towards Establishing a New Field of Archaeological Research. In F. Förster and H. Riemer, eds., *Desert Road Archaeology in Ancient Egypt and Beyond*. Cologne: Heinrich Barth Institut, pp. 19–58.

Robinson, D. (2004). The Mirror of the Sun: Surface, Mineral Applications and Interface in California Rock-Art. In N. Boivin and M. A. Owoc, *Soils, Stones and Symbols: Cultural Perceptions of the Mineral World*, London: UCL Press, pp. 91–105.

Rossi, C. and Ikram, S. (2014). New Kingdom Activities in the Kharga Oasis: The Scribe Userhat Travels Westward. *Journal of Egyptian Archaeology*, 100: 474–478.

Rossi, C. and Ikram, S. (2018). *North Kharga Oasis Survey: Explorations in Egypt's Western Desert*. Leuven: Peeters.

Rothe, R. D., Miller, W. K., and Rapp, G. (2008). *Pharaonic Inscriptions from the Southern Eastern Desert of Egypt*. Winona Lake, Indiana: Eisenbrauns.

Rothenberg, B. (1988). *The Egyptian Mining Temple at Timna*. Researches in the Arabah 1959–1984 1. London: Institute for Archaeo-Metallurgical Studies.

Rothenberg, B. (1993). Timna'. The Hathor Mining Sanctuary: Site 200. In E. Stern, A. Lewinson-Gilboa, and J. Aviram, eds., *The New Encyclopedia of Archaeological Excavations in the Holy Land*. Jerusalem: The Israel Exploration Society and Carta, pp. 1482–1485.

Rummel, U. (2020). Landscape, Tombs, and Sanctuaries: The Interaction of Monuments and Topography in Western Thebes. In C. Geisen, ed., *Ritual Landscape and Performance*. YES 13. New Haven: Yale Egyptology, pp. 89–119.

Sadek, A. I. (1980). *The Amethyst Mining Inscriptions of the Wadi el-Hudi 1*, Warminster: Aris and Phillips.

Schott, S. (1961). *Kanais, der Tempel Sethos I. im Wadi Mia.* Nachrichten der Akademie der Wissenschaften Göttingen I. philologisch-historische Klasse 1961/6. Göttingen: Vandenhoeck & Ruprecht.

Sethe, K. (1908). *Die altaegyptischen Pyramidentexten, vol. 1.*, Leipzig: J. C. Hinrichs'sche Buchhandlung.

Seyfried, K.-J. (1981). *Beiträge zu den Expeditionen des Mittleren Reiches in die Ost-Wüste, HÄB 15*. Hildesheim: Gerstenberg.

Shaw, I. ed. (2000). *The Oxford History of Ancient Egypt*. Oxford: University Press.

Shaw, I. (2006). 'Master of the Roads': Quarrying and Communications Networks in Egypt and Nubia. In B. Mathieu, D. Meeks, and M. Wissa, eds., *L'apport de l'Égypte à l'histoire des techniques*. Cairo: Institut Français d'Archéologie Orientale, pp. 253–266.

Shaw, I. (2010). *Hatnub: Quarrying Travertine in Ancient Egypt*. London: Egypt Exploration Society.

Shaw, I. (2013). "We Went Forth to the Desert Land . . . ": Retracing the Routes between the Nile Valley and the Hatnub Travertine Quarries. In F. Förster and H. Riemer, eds., *Desert Road Archaeology in Ancient Egypt and Beyond*. Cologne: Heinrich-Barth-Institut, pp. 521–532.

Shaw, I., Bloxam, E., Heldal, T., and Storemyr, P. (2010). Quarrying and landscape at Gebel el-Asr in the Old and Middle Kingdoms. In F. Raffaele, M. Nuzzolo, and I. Incordino, eds., *Recent Discoveries and latest researches in Egyptology*. Wiesbaden: Harrassowitz, pp. 293–312.

Sidebotham, S. E. (2011). *Berenike and the Ancient Maritime Spice Route*. Berkeley: University of California Press.

Sidebotham, S. E., H. Barnard, and Pyke, G. (2002). Five Enigmatic Late Roman Settlements in the Eastern Desert. *Journal of Egyptian Archaeology*, 88: 187–225.

Sidebotham, S. E., Hense, M., and Nouwens, H. M. (2008). *The Red Land: the Illustrated Archaeology of Egypt's Eastern Desert*. Cairo: American University in Cairo Press.

Sidebotham, S. E. and Gates-Foster, J. E., eds. (2019). *The Archaeological Survey of the Desert Roads between Berenike and the Nile Valley: Expeditions by the University of Michigan and the University of Delaware* to the Eastern Desert of Egypt, 1987–2015. Boston, MA: American Schools of Oriental Research.

Smith, S. T. (2003). Pharaohs, Feasts, and Foreigners: Cooking, Foodways, and Agency on Ancient Egypt's Southern Frontier. In T. L. Bray, ed., *The Archaeology and Politics of Food and Feasting in Early States and Empires*. New York: Kluwer Academic, pp. 39–64.

Smither, P. C. (1945). The Semnah Despatches. *Journal of Egyptian Archaeology*, 31: 3–10.

Snape, S. (2003). The Emergence of Libya on the Horizon of Egypt. In D. O'Connor and S. Quirke, eds., *Mysterious Lands*. London: UCL Press, pp. 93–106.

Snape, S. (2013). A Stroll along the Corniche? Coastal Routes between the Nile Delta and Cyrenaica in the Late Bronze Age. In F. Förster and H. Riemer, eds., *Desert Road Archaeology in Ancient Egypt and Beyond*. Cologne: Heinrich-Barth-Institut, pp. 439–454.

Snape, S. and Wilson, P. (2007). *Zawiyet Umm el-Rakham I: The Temple and Chapels*. Bolton: Rutherford Press.

Somaglino, C. and Tallet, P. (2014). Une campagne en Nubie sous la Ire dynastie : la scène nagadienne du Gebel Sheikh Suleiman comme prototype et modèle. *NeHeT. Revue numérique d'égyptologie*, n° 1, 1–46.

Somaglino, C. and Tallet, P. (2015). Gebel Sheikh Suleiman: A First Dynasty Relief after All . . .. *Archéo-Nil* 25: 123–134.

Sperveslage, G. (2016). Intercultural Contacts between Egypt and the Arabian Peninsula at the turn of the 2nd to the 2st Millennium BCE. In J. C. Moreno Garcìa. *Dynamics of Production in the Anceint Near East 1300-500 BCE*. Oxford: Oxbow Books, pp. 303–333.

Spiegelberg, W. (1921). *Ägyptische und andere Graffiti (Inschriften und Zeichnungen) aus der thebanischen Nekropolis*, Volume 2. Heidelberg: Carl Winters Universitätsbuchhandlung.

Stauder, A. (2010). The Earliest Egyptian Writing. In C. Woods, ed., *Visible Language, Inventions of Writing in the Ancient Middle East and Beyond*. Chicago: The Oriental Institute of the University of Chicago, pp. 137–148.

Stauder, A. (f.c.) On the Way to Writing. The U-j Inscriptions (3200 BCE) Reconsidered, forthcoming.

Storemyr, P., Bloxam, E., Heldal, T., and Kelany, A. (2013). Ancient Desert and Quarry Roads on the West Bank of the Nile in the First Cataract Region. In F. Förster and H. Riemer, eds., *Desert Road Archaeology in Ancient Egypt and Beyond*. Cologne: Heinrich-Barth-Institut, pp. 399–423.

Suková, L. (2011). *The Rock Art of Lower Nubia (Czechoslovak Concession)*. Prague: Charles University, Faculty of Arts.

Sweeney, D. (2014). Self-Representation in Old Kingdom Quarrying Inscriptions at Wadi Hammamat. *Journal Egyptian Archaeology*, 100: 275–291.

Sweeney, D. (2018). The Inscription of Ramessesemperre in Context. In E. Ben-Yosef, ed., *Mining for Ancient Copper: Essays in Memory of Beno Rothenberg*. University Park, PA: Eisenbrauns, pp. 109–117.

Taçon, P. S. C. (2004). Ochre, Clay, Stone and Art: the Symbolic Importance of Minerals as Life-Force among Aboriginal Peoples of Northern and Central Australia. In N. Boivin and M. A. Owoc, eds., *Soils, Stones and Symbols: Cultural Perceptions of the Mineral World*, London: UCL Press.

Tallet, P. (2015a). *La zone minière pharaonique du Sud-Sinaï – II, Les inscriptions pré- et protodynastiques du Ouadi 'Ameyra (CCIS nos 273-335)*. Cairo: Institut Français d'Archéologie Orientale.

Tallet, P. (2015b). *La zone minière pharaonique du Sud-Sinaï – III, Les expéditions égyptiennes dans la zone minière du Sud- Sinaï du prédynastique à la fin de la XXe dynastie*. Cairo: Institut Français d'Archéologie Orientale.

Tallet, P. (2016). The Egyptians on the Red Sea Shore during the Pharaonic Era. In M. F. Boussac, J. F. Salles, and J. B. Yon, eds., *Ports of the Ancient Indian Ocean*. Delhi: Primus Books, pp. 3–19.

Tallet, P. (2016/2017). D'Ayn Soukhna à la peninsula du Sinai: le mode opératoire des expeditions égyptiennes à la fin de la 12e dynastie. *Cahiers de Recherches de l'Institut de Papyrologie et d'Égyptologie de Lille*, 31: 179–198.

Tallet, P. and Marouard, G. (2016). The Harbour Facilities of King Khufu on the Red Sea Shore: The Wadi al-Jarf/Tell Ras Budran System. *Journal of the American Research Center in Egypt*, 52: 135–177.

Tallet, P. and Mahfouz, E. (2012). *The Red Sea in Pharaonic Times, Recent Discoveries along the Red Sea Coast*. Cairo: Institut Français d'Archéologie Orientale.

Tallet, G. and Sauzeau, T., eds. (2018). *Mer et desert de l'Antiquité à nos journs: approaches croisées*. Rennes: Presses universitaires de Rennes.

Thiry, J. (1995). *Le Sahara Libyen dans l'Afrique du Nord Medievale*. Leuven: Uitgeverij Peeters.

Trigger, B. G. (1996) Toshka and Arminna in the New Kingdom. In P. Der Manuelian, ed., *Studies in Honor of William Kelly Simpson*. Boston: Museum of Fine Arts, pp. 801–810.

Váhala, F. and Červicek, P. (1999). *Katalog der Felsbilder aus der tschecho-slowakischen Konzession in Nubie*, volume 1, Prague: Verlag Karolinum.

Valbelle, D. and Bonnet, C. (1996). *Le sanctuaire d'Hathor, maîtresse de la turqoiuse: Sérabit el-Khadim au Moyen Empire*, Paris: Picard Editeur.

Vandekerckhove, H. and Müller-Wollermann, R. (2001). *Die Felsinschriften des Wadi Hilâl, Elkab 6*. Turnhout: Brepols.

Van Pelt, W. P. (2013). Revising Egypt-Nubian Relations in New Kingdom Lower Nubia: From Egyptianization to Cultural Entanglement. *Cambridge Archaeological Journal* 23/3: 523–550.

Van Siclen, C. (1997). Remarks on the Gebel Agg Inscription. In J. Aksamit, *et al.*, eds., *Essays in Honour of Prof. Dr. Jadwiga Lipińska*. Warsaw Egyptological Studies 1. Warsaw: National Museum, pp. 409–416.

Vasáros, Z. (2010). Architectural Remains – Introduction. In U. Luft, ed., *Bi'r Minayh, Report on the Survey 1998–2004*. Budapest: Archaeolingua Alapítvány, pp. 197–213.

Vercoutter, J. (1970). *Mirgissa*. Paris: P. Geuthner.

Vittmann, G. (2003). *Ägypten und die Fremden im ersten vorchristlichen Jahrtausend*. Mainz: Verlag Philipp von Zabern.

Vogel, C. (2004). *Ägyptische Festungen und Garnisonen bis zum Ende des Mittleren Reiches*. Hildesheim: Gerstenberg.

Vogel, C. (2013). Keeping the Enemy Out – Egyptian Fortifications of the Third and Second Millennium BC. In F. Jesse and C. Vogel, eds., *The Power of Walls – Fortifications in Ancient Northeastern Africa*. Cologne: Heinrich-Barth-Institut, pp. 73–100.

Vogel, C. (2015). Policing and Site Protection, Guard Posts, and Enclosure Walls. In R. H. Wilkinson and K. R. Weeks, eds., *The Oxford Handbook of the Valley of the Kings*. Oxford: Oxford University Press, pp. 433–447.

Warfe, A. and Ricketts, S. M. (2019). The Sheikh Muftah Cultural Unit: An Overview of Oasis/Desert Habitation during the 4th and 3rd Millennia with Comments on Future Research Directions. In G. E. Bowen and C. A. Hope, eds., *The Oasis Papers 9: A Tribute to Anthony J. Mills after Forty Years in Dakhleh Oasis*. Oxford: Oxbow Books, pp. 95–108.

Waterton, E. (2013). Landscape and Non-Representational Theories. In P. Howard, I. Thompson, and E. Waterton, eds., *The Routledge Companion to Landscape Studies*, London: Routledge, pp. 66–75.

Wegner, J. (2017/2018). The Stela of Idudju-Iker, Foremost-One of the Chiefs of Wawat: New Evidence on the Conquest of Thinis under Wahankh Antef II. *Revue d'égyptologie*, 68: 153–209.

Welvaert, E. (2002). The Fossils of Qau el Kebir and their Role in the Mythology of the 10th Nome of Upper-Egypt. *Zeitschrift für ägyptische Sprache und Altertumskunde*, 129: 166–183.

Wengrow, D. (2011). The Invention of Writing in Egypt. In E. Teeter, ed., *Before the Pyramids: The Origins of Egyptian Civilization*. Chicago: The Oriental Institute of the University of Chicago, pp. 99–103.

Whitley, D. S. (1998). Finding Rain in the Desert: Landscape, Gender and Far Western North American Rock-Art. In C. Chippendale and P. S. C. Taçon, eds., *The Archaeology of Rock-Art*, Cambridge: Cambridge University Press, pp. 11–29.

Wilkinson, T. (1999). *Early Dynastic Egypt*. London: Routledge.

Willeitner, J. (2003). *Die ägyptischen Oasen: Städte, Tempel und Gräber in der Libyschen Wüste*. Mainz: Zabern.

Williams, B. (1986). *Excavations between Abu Simbel and the Sudan Frontier, Part 1: The A-Group Royal Cemetery at Qustul: Cemetery L. Oriental Institute Nubian Expedition 3*. Chicago: Oriental Institute.

Williams, B. (2006). *The Cave Shrine and the Gebel*. In E. Czerny, *et al.*, eds., *Timelines, Studies in Honour of Manfred Bietak*. Leuven: Peeters, pp.149–158.

Williams, B. and Logan, T. (1987). The Metropolitan Museum Knife Handle and Aspects of Pharaonic Imagery before Narmer. *Journal of Near Eastern Studies*, 46: 245–285.

Winkler, H. (1938). *Rock-Drawings of Southern Upper Egypt I*. London: Egypt Exploration Society.

Winkler, H. (1939). *Rock-Drawings of Southern Upper Egypt II*. London: Egypt Exploration Society.

Winlock, H. E. (1947). *The Rise and Fall of the Middle Kingdom in Thebes*, New York: The Macmillan Company.

Wreszinski, W. (1935). *Atlas zur altaegyptischen Kulturgeschichte*. Vol. 2. Leipzig: J. C. Hinrichs.

Wuttmann, M., Briois, F., Midant-Reynes, F., and Dachy, T. (2012). Dating the End of the Neolithic in an Eastern Sahara Oasis: Modeling Absolute Chronology. *Radiocarbon* 54: 305–318.

Wylie, J. (2007) *Landscape*. London: Routledge.

Yamamoto, K. (2015). Abydos and Osiris: The Terrace of the Great God. In A. Oppenheim, *et al.*, eds., *Ancient Egypt Transformed: The Middle Kingdom*. New York: Metropolitan Museum of Art, pp. 250–253.

Young, G. K. (2001). *Rome's Eastern Trade: International Commerce and Imperial Policy, 31 BC-AD 305*. London: Routledge.

Yoyotte, J. (2010). La statue égyptienne de Darius. In J. Perrot, ed., *Le Palais de Darius à Suse: une résidence royale sur la route de Persépolis à Babylone*. Paris: PUPS, pp. 256–299.

Žaba, Z. (1974). *The Rock Inscriptions of Lower Nubia*. Prague: Universita Karlova.

Acknowledgments

I thank Profs. Juan Carlos Moreno Garcia and Gianluca Miniaci for the invitation to contribute to the Cambridge Elements series. I have much enjoyed attempting, however imperfectly, to encapsulate approximately three decades of work in the Western and Eastern Deserts of Egypt and place it in the larger context of ancient Egyptian approaches to the forbidding landscapes east and west of the Nile Valley, from routine administration to religious activities. For the permission to carry out this work, and for years of support and assistance, I thank all of my colleagues, past and present, in what is now the Ministry of Antiquities in Egypt. In addition to various smaller grants, devoted to the work, much of the material appearing in this volume was supported by grants from the National Endowment for the Humanities (an independent federal agency of the United States Government), and the William K. and Marilyn M. Simpson Endowment for Egyptology at Yale University.

Many colleagues around the world have contributed at various times and in a variety of ways to the field work and research included in the current volume; with apologies for not naming everyone, I shall try to list at least a few. Deborah Darnell was a founding co-director of the Theban Desert Road Survey, and I thank her for her significant contributions to the mission and its discoveries, several of which are referenced here; she continues the work of the Theban Desert Road Survey, and will publish final editions of several sites referenced here (such as SWA-1). I would like to thank Stan Hendrickx and Maria Gatto for fruitful discussions of Predynastic and Protodynastic rock art; Frank Forster and Heiko Riemer for insights into far Western Desert caravan routes; in recent years, Dorian Vanhulle and Axelle Brémont-Bellini, have undertaken important analyses of rock art as members of the Elkab Desert Survey Project. Vincent Morel and Jean-Guillaume Olette-Pelettier have kindly shared the result of their exciting work with Prof. Annie Gasse in the Wadi Hammamat, and I thank them for many interesting discussions. The late Dr. Dirk Huyge was kind enough to invite me to begin the Elkab Desert Survey, which his successor Wouter Claes continues to support and encourage. The detailed maps and figures within this volume would not have been possible without the skill of Alberto Urcia, whose pioneering digital rock art recording technique has transformed our field work. My archaeological and epigraphic work in the Eastern and Western Deserts would not have been possible without the logistical and automotive expertise of Abdou Abdullah Hassan, to whom I dedicate this volume.

For Abdou Abdullah Hassan

Cambridge Elements ☰

Ancient Egypt in Context

Gianluca Miniaci

University of Pisa

Gianluca Miniaci is Associate Professor in Egyptology at the University of Pisa, Honorary Researcher at the Institute of Archaeology, UCL – London, and Chercheur associé at the École Pratique des Hautes Études, Paris. He is currently co-director of the archaeological mission at Zawyet Sultan (Menya, Egypt). His main research interest focuses on the social history and the dynamics of material culture in the Middle Bronze Age Egypt and its interconnections between the Levant, Aegean, and Nubia.

Juan Carlos Moreno García

CNRS, Paris

Juan Carlos Moreno García (PhD in Egyptology, 1995) is a CNRS senior researcher at the University of Paris IV-Sorbonne, as well as lecturer on social and economic history of ancient Egypt at the École des Hautes Études en Sciences Sociales (EHESS) in Paris. He has published extensively on the administration, socio-economic history, and landscape organization of ancient Egypt, usually in a comparative perspective with other civilizations of the ancient world, and has organized several conferences on these topics.

Anna Stevens

University of Cambridge and Monash University

Anna Stevens is a research archaeologist with a particular interest in how material culture and urban space can shed light on the lives of the non-elite in ancient Egypt. She is Senior Research Associate at the McDonald Institute for Archaeological Research and Assistant Director of the Amarna Project (both University of Cambridge).

About the Series

The aim of this Elements series is to offer authoritative but accessible overviews of foundational and emerging topics in the study of ancient Egypt, along with comparative analyses, translated into a language comprehensible to non-specialists. Its authors will take a step back and connect ancient Egypt to the world around, bringing ancient Egypt to the attention of the broader humanities community and leading Egyptology in new directions.

Cambridge Elements ☰

Ancient Egypt in Context

CPSIA information can be obtained
at www.ICGtesting.com
Printed in the USA
LVHW021141260721
693681LV00011B/1135